McGraw-Hill's
CHINESE
ILLUSTRATED
DICTIONARY

New York   Chicago   San Francisco   Lisbon   London   Madrid   Mexico City
Milan   New Delhi   San Juan   Seoul   Singapore   Sydney   Toronto

3 4 5 6 7 8 9 10 11 12 13 14 15 16 17 18 19 20 21   CTP/CTP 19 18 17 16 15 14

ISBN 978-0-07-161590-7 (book and CD set)
MHID   0-07-161590-3 (book and CD set)

ISBN 978-0-07-161591-4 (book for set)
MHID   0-07-161591-1 (book for set)

Library of Congress Control Number: 2008935413

McGraw-Hill books are available at special quantity discounts to use as premiums and sales promotions or for use in corporate training programs. To contact a representative, please visit the Contact Us pages at www.mhprofessional.com.

MP3 Disk

The accompanying disk contains MP3 recordings of all terms presented in this dictionary. These files can be played on all MP3 players.
   For optimum use on the iPod:

1. Open iTunes on your computer.
2. Insert the disk into your computer and open via My Computer.
3. Drag the folder "Copy to iTunes Music Library" into Music in the iTunes menu. For older/slower computers, it is suggested that you first open this folder and drag the folders within to iTunes separately.
4. Sync your iPod with iTunes and eject the iPod.
5. Locate the recordings on your iPod by following this path:
   Main menu: **Menu**
   Music menu: **Artists**
   Artist menu: **Chinese Illustrated Dictionary**
6. If you experience difficulties, check the Read Me file on the disk.

Contents

How to Use This Book

It is suggested that you listen to the audio recordings when using this book. It will make your learning more efficient.

Category title shown in English

Unit title including English and simplified Chinese

Category title shown in simplified Chinese

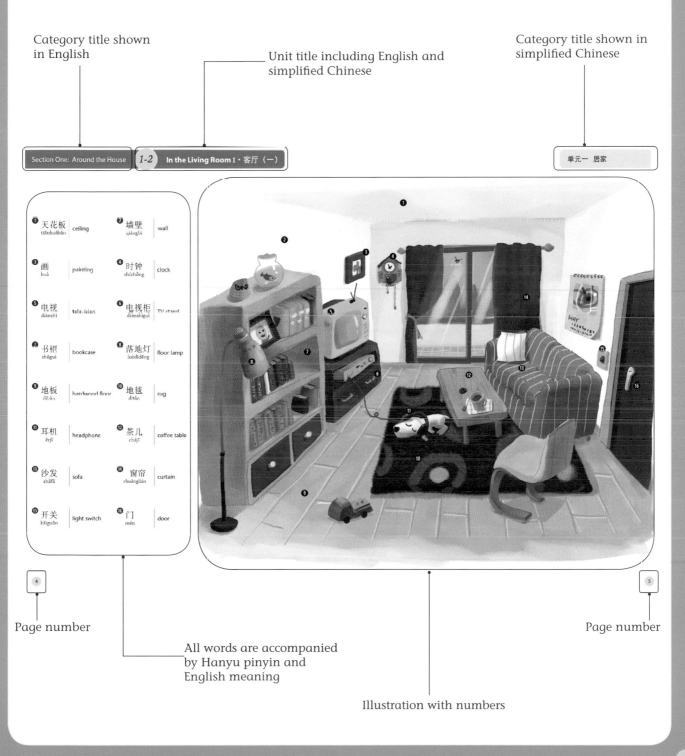

Section One: Around the House   1-2   In the Living Room I · 客厅（一）

单元一 居家

❶ 天花板 tiānhuābǎn	ceiling	❷ 墙壁 qiángbì	wall
❸ 画 huà	painting	❹ 时钟 shízhōng	clock
❺ 电视 diànshì	television	❻ 电视柜 diànshìguì	TV stand
❼ 书柜 shūguì	bookcase	❽ 落地灯 luòdìdēng	floor lamp
❾ 地板 dìbǎn	hardwood floor	❿ 地毯 dìtǎn	rug
⓫ 耳机 ěrjī	headphone	⓬ 茶几 chájī	coffee table
⓭ 沙发 shāfā	sofa	⓮ 窗帘 chuānglián	curtain
⓯ 开关 kāiguān	light switch	⓰ 门 mén	door

4

5

Page number

Page number

All words are accompanied by Hanyu pinyin and English meaning

Illustration with numbers

1 大楼 | building
dàlóu

2 铁窗 | iron window
tiěchuāng

3 游泳池 | swimming pool
yóuyǒngchí

4 大门 | main gate
dàmén

5 保安 | security guard
bǎo'ān

6 公寓 | apartment
gōngyù

7 阳台 | balcony
yángtái

8 顶楼 | top floor
dǐnglóu

9 楼梯 | stair
lóutī

10 车库 | garage
chēkù

11 院子 | yard
yuànzi

12 信箱 | mailbox
xìnxiāng

❶ 天花板 ceiling
tiānhuābǎn

❷ 墙壁 wall
qiángbì

❸ 画 painting
huà

❹ 时钟 clock
shízhōng

❺ 电视 television
diànshì

❻ 电视柜 TV stand
diànshìguì

❼ 书柜 bookcase
shūguì

❽ 落地灯 floor lamp
luòdìdēng

❾ 地板 hardwood floor
dìbǎn

❿ 地毯 rug
dìtǎn

⓫ 耳机 headphones
ěrjī

⓬ 茶几 coffee table
chájī

⓭ 沙发 sofa
shāfā

⓮ 窗帘 curtain
chuānglián

⓯ 开关 light switch
kāiguān

⓰ 门 door
mén

❶ 扶手椅 fúshǒuyǐ	armchair	❷ 躺椅 tǎngyǐ	recliner	❸ 摇椅 yáoyǐ	rocking chair
❹ 小茶几 xiǎochájī	end table	❺ 电话 diànhuà	telephone	❻ 花瓶 huāpíng	vase
❼ 垃圾桶 lājītǒng	trash can	❽ 空调 kōngtiáo	air conditioner		

⑨ 暖炉
nuǎnlú | space heater

⑩ 电扇
diànshàn | fan

⑪ 音响
yīnxiǎng | stereo

⑫ DVD | DVD player

⑬ 遥控器
yáokòngqì | remote control

⑭ 吸尘器
xīchénqì | vacuum cleaner

⑮ 电话录音机
diànhuà lùyīnjī | answering machine

❶ 台式电脑 | desktop computer
táishì diànnǎo

❷ 笔记本电脑 | notebook computer
bǐjìběn diànnǎo

❸ CRT显示器 | CRT monitor
CRT-xiǎnshìqì

❹ 液晶显示器 | LCD monitor
yèjīng xiǎnshìqì

❺ 主板 | motherboard
zhǔbǎn

❻ 中央处理器 | CPU
zhōngyāng chǔlǐqì

❼ 内存 | RAM
nèicún

❽ 硬盘 | hard disk
yìngpán

❾ 网卡 | network adapter card
wǎngkǎ

❿ 调制解调器 | modem
tiáozhì jiětiáoqì

⓫ 鼠标 | mouse
shǔbiāo

⓬ 鼠标垫 | mouse pad
shǔbiāodiàn

⓭ 键盘 | keyboard
jiànpán

⓮ 光驱 | DVD-ROM drive
guāngqū

⓯ 光盘 | DVD
guāngpán

16 刻录机 | CD burner
kèlùjī

17 集线器 | hub
jíxiànqì

18 音箱 | speaker
yīnxiāng

19 软盘 | floppy disk
ruǎnpán

20 U盘 | flash drive
U-pán

21 扫瞄仪 | scanner
sǎomiáoyí

22 摄像头 | webcam
shèxiàngtóu

23 打印机 | printer
dǎyìnjī

24 传真机 | fax machine
chuánzhēnjī

25 复印机 | photocopier
fùyìnjī

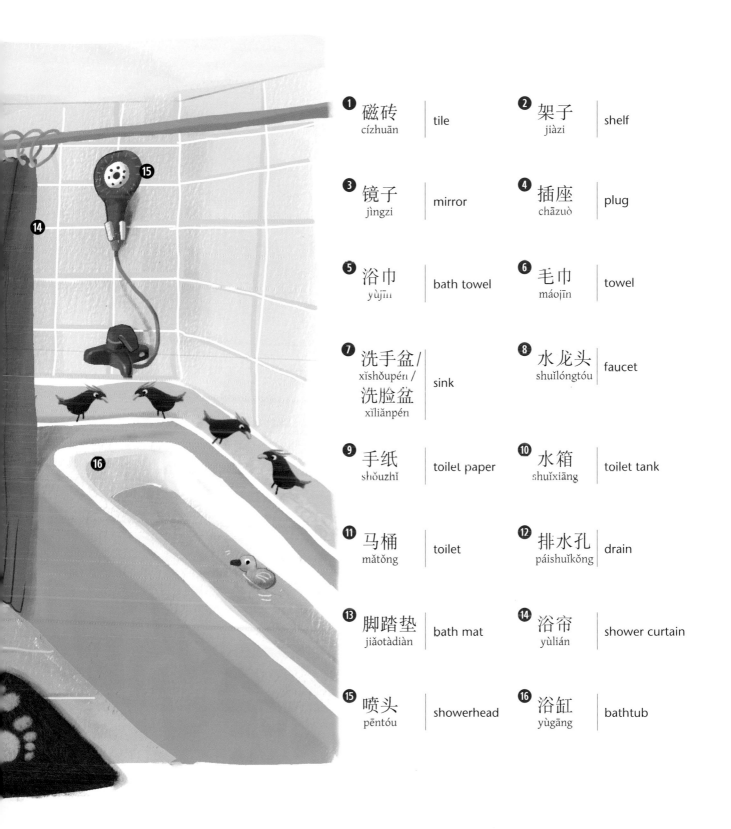

1 磁砖
cízhuān | tile

2 架子
jiàzi | shelf

3 镜子
jìngzi | mirror

4 插座
chāzuò | plug

5 浴巾
yùjīn | bath towel

6 毛巾
máojīn | towel

7 洗手盆 /
xǐshǒupén /
洗脸盆
xǐliǎnpén | sink

8 水龙头
shuǐlóngtóu | faucet

9 手纸
shǒuzhǐ | toilet paper

10 水箱
shuǐxiāng | toilet tank

11 马桶
mǎtǒng | toilet

12 排水孔
páishuǐkǒng | drain

13 脚踏垫
jiǎotàdiàn | bath mat

14 浴帘
yùlián | shower curtain

15 喷头
pēntóu | showerhead

16 浴缸
yùgāng | bathtub

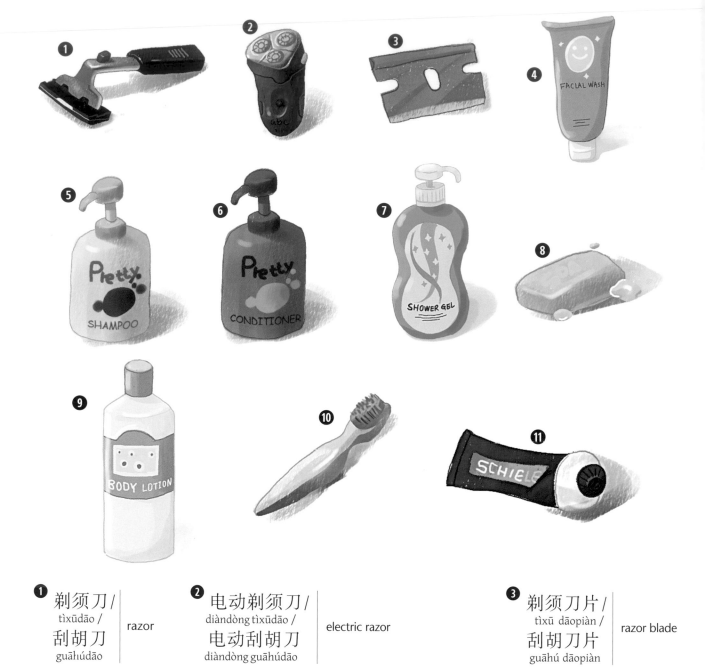

1 剃须刀 /
tìxūdāo /
刮胡刀
guāhúdāo | razor

2 电动剃须刀 /
diàndòng tìxūdāo /
电动刮胡刀
diàndòng guāhúdāo | electric razor

3 剃须刀片 /
tìxū dāopiàn /
刮胡刀片
guāhú dāopiàn | razor blade

4 洗面奶
xǐmiànnǎi | facial wash

5 洗发水 /
xǐfàshuǐ /
洗发液
xǐfàyè | shampoo

6 润发液 /
rùnfàyè /
润发露
rùnfàlù | conditioner

7 沐浴液
mùyùyè | shower gel

8 香皂
xiāngzào | soap

9 润肤露
rùnfūlù | body lotion

10 牙刷
yáshuā | toothbrush

11 牙膏
yágāo | toothpaste

⑫ 吹风机
chuīfēngjī | blow-dryer

⑬ 梳子
shūzi | hairbrush

⑭ 棉花棒
miánhuābàng | cotton swab

⑮ 指甲刀
zhǐjiǎdāo | nail clipper

⑯ 面巾纸
miànjīnzhǐ | facial tissue

⑰ 香水
xiāngshuǐ | perfume

⑱ 体重秤
tǐzhòngchèng | scale

⑲ 洗衣篮
xǐyīlán | laundry basket

⑳ 浴袍
yùpáo | bathrobe

㉑ 浴帽
yùmào | shower cap

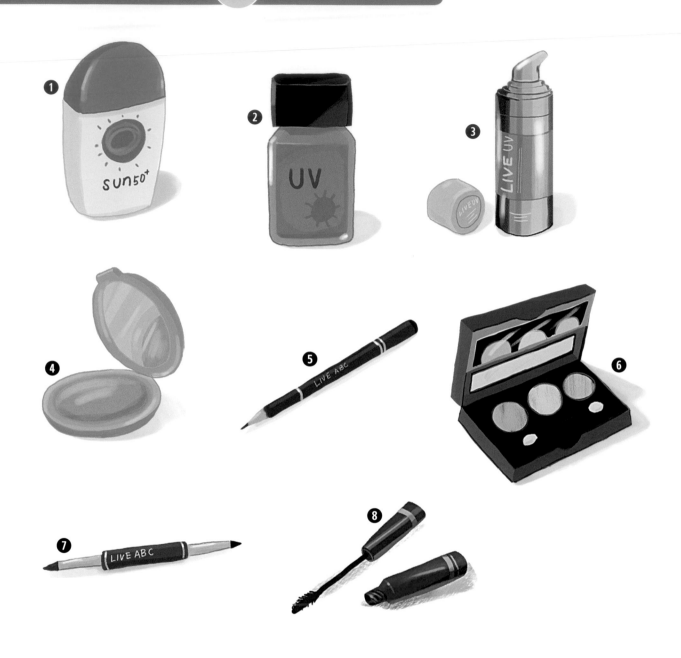

❶ 防晒油 | sunscreen
fángshàiyóu

❷ 隔离霜 | pre-makeup
gélíshuāng | cream

❸ 粉底液 | moisture
fěndǐyè | foundation

❹ 粉饼 | compact
fěnbǐng | foundation

❺ 眉笔 | eyebrow
méibǐ | pencil

❻ 眼影 | eye shadow
yǎnyǐng

❼ 眼线笔 | eye pencil
yǎnxiànbǐ

❽ 睫毛膏 | mascara
jiémáogāo

⑨ 睫毛夹 jiémáojiá | eyelash curler

⑩ 腮红 sāihóng | blush

⑪ 刷子 shuāzi | brush

⑫ 口红 kǒuhóng | lipstick

⑬ 指甲油 zhǐjiǎyóu | nail polish

⑭ 卸妆油 xièzhuāngyóu | makeup remover

⑮ 面膜 miànmó | mask

1 闹钟
nàozhōng | alarm clock

2 相框
xiàngkuàng | picture frame

3 台灯
táidēng | lamp

4 床头几
chuángtóujī | nightstand

5 床头柜
chuángtóuguì | headboard cabinet

6 枕头
zhěntou | pillow

7 双人床
shuāngrénchuáng | double bed

8 床垫
chuángdiàn | mattress

9 床单
chuángdān | sheet

10 被子
bèizi | comforter

11 拖鞋
tuōxié | slippers

12 汗衫
hànshān | undershirt

13 脚凳
jiǎodèng | footstool

14 五斗柜
wǔdǒuguì | chest of drawers

15 书档
shūdǎng | bookend

16 衣橱
yīchú | wardrobe

17 化妆品
huàzhuāngpǐn | cosmetics

18 梳妆台
shūzhuāngtái | vanity

Additional Information: Kinds of Beds	
1. 单人床 dānrénchuáng	single bed
2. 沙发床 shāfāchuáng	sofa bed

① 洗衣液 | laundry detergent
xǐyīyè

② 柔顺剂 | fabric softener
róushùnjì

③ 漂白粉 / | bleach
piǎobáifěn /
漂白液
piǎobáiyè

④ 衣架 | hanger
yījià

⑤ 夹子 | clothes pin
jiázi

⑥ 线 | thread
xiàn

⑦ 烫衣板 | ironing board
tàngyībǎn

⑧ 熨斗 | iron
yùndǒu

⑨ 抹布 mābù	rag	⑩ 洗衣网 xǐyīwǎng	laundry bag	⑪ 扫把 sàobǎ	broom	⑫ 簸箕 bòji	dustpan
⑬ 拖把 tuōbǎ	mop	⑭ 洗衣机 xǐyījī	washing machine	⑮ 烘干机 hōnggānjī	dryer		

1 冰箱
bīngxiāng
| refrigerator

2 围裙
wéiqún
| apron

3 咖啡壶
kāfēihú
| coffee maker

4 抽油烟机
chōuyóuyānjī
| range fan

5 碗柜
wǎnguì
| cupboard

6 微波炉
wēibōlú
| microwave oven

7 碗架
wǎnjià
| dish rack

8 勺子
sháozi
| ladle

9 菜刀
càidāo
| cleaver

10 平底锅
píngdǐguō
| pan

11 煤气炉
méiqìlú
| gas stove

12 炒菜锅
chǎocàiguō
| wok

13 水槽
shuǐcáo
| sink

14 操作台
cāozuòtái
| counter

15 菜板子
càibǎnzi
| cutting board

16 烘碗机
hōngwǎnjī
| dish dryer

17 烤箱
kǎoxiāng
| oven

18 柜子
guìzi
| cabinet

19 榨汁机
zhàzhījī
| blender

20 电饭锅
diànfànguō
| rice cooker

21 电热水壶
diànrèshuǐhú
| electric water boiler

22 烤面包机
kǎomiànbāojī
| toaster

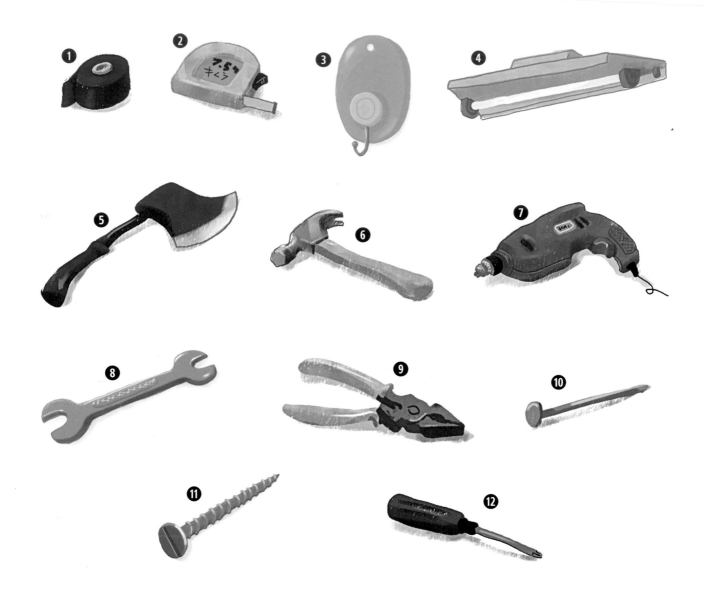

❶ 胶带 jiāodài	tape	❷ 皮尺 píchǐ	tape measure	❸ 挂钩 guàgōu	hook	❹ 日光灯 rìguāngdēng	fluorescent light
❺ 斧头 fǔtou	ax	❻ 榔头 lángtou	hammer	❼ 电钻 diànzuàn	electric drill	❽ 扳手 bānshou	wrench
❾ 钳子 qiánzi	pliers	❿ 铁钉 tiědīng	nail	⓫ 螺丝 luósī	screw	⓬ 螺丝刀 luósīdāo	screwdriver

⑬ 手电筒 shǒudiàntǒng	flashlight	⑭ 工具箱 gōngjùxiāng	toolbox	⑮ 油漆 yóuqī	paint	⑯ 油漆刷 yóuqīshuā	paintbrush
⑰ 油漆滚筒 yóuqī gǔntǒng	paint roller	⑱ 梯子 tīzi	ladder	⑲ 铲子 chǎnzi	shovel	⑳ 刷子 shuāzi	scrubbing brush
㉑ 水桶 shuǐtǒng	bucket	㉒ 海绵 hǎimián	sponge					

❶ 吸地 — vacuum
xī dì

❷ 扫地 — sweep the floor
sǎodì

❸ 洗 — wash
xǐ

❹ 洗衣 — do the laundry
xǐyī

❺ 熨衣服 — iron the clothes
yùn yīfu

❻ 缝 — sew
féng

❼ 编织 — knit
biānzhī

❽ 吃 — eat
chī

❾ 喝 — drink
hē

❿ 做饭 — cook
zuòfàn

⓫ 洗碗 — wash the dishes
xǐ wǎn

⓬ 睡觉 — sleep
shuìjiào

⓭ 起床 — get up
qǐchuáng

⓮ 刷牙 — brush one's teeth
shuā yá

⓯ 洗脸 — wash one's face
xǐ liǎn

16 洗澡 xǐzǎo	take a shower	**17** 穿 chuān	wear (clothing)	**18** 戴 dài

16 洗澡 xǐzǎo — take a shower

17 穿 chuān — wear (clothing)

18 戴 dài — wear (accessories)

19 脱 tuō — take off

20 打电话 dǎ diànhuà — make a phone call

21 浇花 jiāo huā — water the plants

22 倒垃圾 dào lājī — take out the garbage

23 打开 dǎkāi — open / turn on

24 关上 guānshàng — close / turn off

2-1 **People · 人**

❶ 男人 | man
nánrén

❷ 女人 | woman
nǚrén

❸ 老先生 | aged man
lǎoxiānsheng

❹ 老太太 | aged woman
lǎotàitai

❺ 中年人 | middle-ager
zhōngnián rén

6 男孩儿 | boy
nánháir

7 女孩儿 | girl
nǚháir

8 青少年 | teenager
qīngshàonián

9 孕妇 | pregnant woman
yùnfù

10 幼儿 | toddler
yòu'ér

11 小孩儿 | child
xiǎoháir

12 婴儿 | baby
yīng'ér

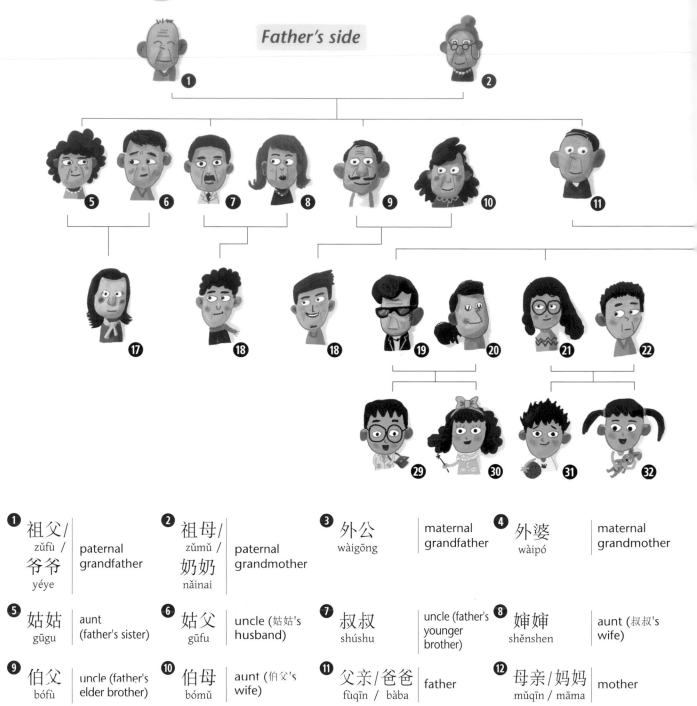

Father's side

❶ 祖父 / zǔfù / 爷爷 yéye	paternal grandfather	❷ 祖母 / zǔmǔ / 奶奶 nǎinai	paternal grandmother	❸ 外公 wàigōng	maternal grandfather	❹ 外婆 wàipó	maternal grandmother
❺ 姑姑 gūgu	aunt (father's sister)	❻ 姑父 gūfu	uncle (姑姑's husband)	❼ 叔叔 shúshu	uncle (father's younger brother)	❽ 婶婶 shěnshen	aunt (叔叔's wife)
❾ 伯父 bófù	uncle (father's elder brother)	❿ 伯母 bómǔ	aunt (伯父's wife)	⓫ 父亲 / 爸爸 fùqīn / bàba	father	⓬ 母亲 / 妈妈 mǔqīn / māma	mother
⓭ 舅舅 jiùjiu	uncle (mother's brother)	⓮ 舅妈 jiùmā	aunt (舅舅's wife)	⓯ 姨妈 yímā	aunt (mother's sister)	⓰ 姨丈 yízhàng	uncle (姨妈's husband)
⓱ 表哥 / 表姐 / biǎogē / biǎojiě / 表弟 / 表妹 biǎodì / biǎomèi	cousin (姑姑, 舅舅 and 姨妈's children)	⓲ 堂哥 / 堂姐 / tánggē / tángjiě / 堂弟 / 堂妹 tángdì / tángmèi	cousin (伯父 and 叔叔's children)	⓳ 哥哥 gēge	elder brother	⓴ 嫂子 sǎozi	sister-in-law (哥哥's wife)

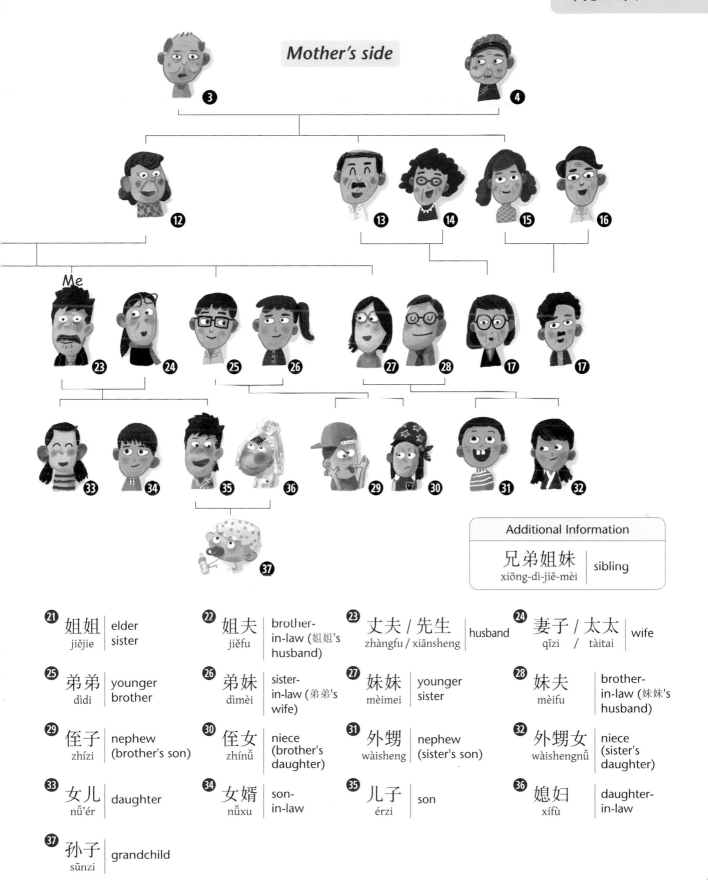

Mother's side

Me

Additional Information

兄弟姐妹 xiōng-dì-jiě-mèi	sibling

㉑ 姐姐 | elder
jiějie | sister

㉒ 姐夫 | brother-
jiěfu | in-law (姐姐's
| husband)

㉓ 丈夫 / 先生 | husband
zhàngfu / xiānsheng |

㉔ 妻子 / 太太 | wife
qīzi / tàitai |

㉕ 弟弟 | younger
dìdi | brother

㉖ 弟妹 | sister-
dìmèi | in-law (弟弟's
| wife)

㉗ 妹妹 | younger
mèimei | sister

㉘ 妹夫 | brother-
mèifu | in-law (妹妹's
| husband)

㉙ 侄子 | nephew
zhízi | (brother's son)

㉚ 侄女 | niece
zhínǚ | (brother's
| daughter)

㉛ 外甥 | nephew
wàisheng | (sister's son)

㉜ 外甥女 | niece
wàishengnǚ | (sister's
| daughter)

㉝ 女儿 | daughter
nǚ'ér |

㉞ 女婿 | son-
nǚxu | in-law

㉟ 儿子 | son
érzi |

㊱ 媳妇 | daughter-
xífù | in-law

㊲ 孙子 | grandchild
sūnzi |

❶ 业务员 yèwùyuán	salesman	❷ 助理 zhùlǐ	assistant	❸ 秘书 mìshū	secretary	❹ 经理 jīnglǐ	manager
❺ 记者 jìzhě	reporter	❻ 老师 lǎoshī	teacher	❼ 教授 jiàoshòu	professor	❽ 公务员 gōngwùyuán	public servant
❾ 警察 jǐngchá	policeman	❿ 消防员 xiāofángyuán	firefighter	⓫ 军人 jūnrén	soldier	⓬ 司机 sījī	driver

⑬ 飞行员 fēixíngyuán | pilot

⑭ 农民 nóngmín | farmer

⑮ 渔夫 yúfū | fisherman

⑯ 厨师 chúshī | chef

⑰ 建筑师 jiànzhùshī | architect

⑱ 技工 jìgōng | mechanic

⑲ 木匠 mùjiang | carpenter

⑳ 工人 gōngrén | laborer

㉑ 水电工 shuǐdiàngōng | plumber

❶ 医生
yīshēng | doctor

❷ 护士
hùshi | nurse

❸ 科学家
kēxuéjiā | scientist

❹ 工程师
gōngchéngshī | engineer

❺ 政治家
zhèngzhìjiā | politician

❻ 商人
shāngrén | businessman

❼ 企业家
qǐyèjiā | entrepreneur

❽ 律师
lǜshī | lawyer

❾ 法官
fǎguān | judge

❿ 导游
dǎoyóu | tour guide

11 中介 | broker /
zhōngjiè | agent

12 男演员 | actor
nányǎnyuán

13 女演员 | actress
nǚyǎnyuán

14 歌手 | singer
gēshǒu

15 发型设计师 | hairstylist
fàxíngshèjìshī

16 艺术家 | artist
yìshùjiā

17 音乐家 | musician
yīnyuèjiā

18 舞蹈家 | dancer
wǔdǎojiā

19 雕塑家 | sculptor
diāosùjiā

20 运动员 | athlete
yùndòngyuán

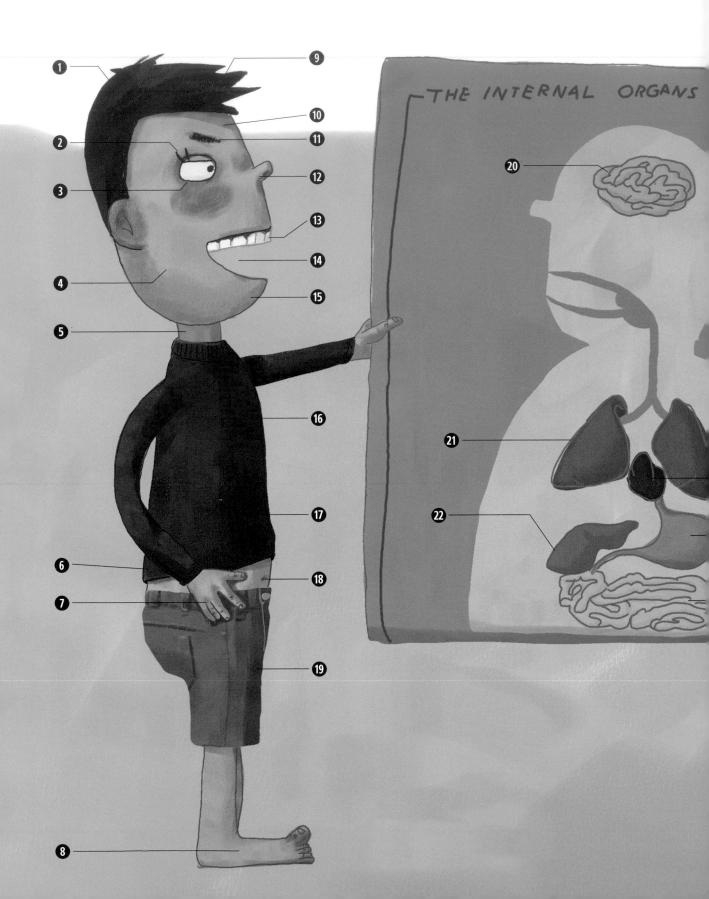

THE INTERNAL ORGANS

1 头 tóu | head

2 眼睫毛 yǎnjiémáo | eyelash

3 眼睛 yǎnjing | eye

4 脸颊 liǎnjiá | cheek

5 脖子 bózi | neck

6 腰 yāo | waist

7 手 shǒu | hand

8 脚 jiǎo | foot

9 头发 tóufa | hair

10 额头 étóu | forehead

11 眉毛 méimao | eyebrow

12 鼻子 bízi | nose

13 牙齿 yáchǐ | tooth

14 嘴巴 zuǐba | mouth

15 下巴 xiàba | chin

16 胸部 xiōngbù | chest

17 肚子 dùzi | belly

18 肚脐 dùqí | navel

19 大腿 dàtuǐ | thigh

20 脑 nǎo | brain

21 肺 fèi | lung

22 肝 gān | liver

23 心脏 xīnzàng | heart

24 胃 wèi | stomach

25 肠 cháng | intestine

❶ 快乐 | happy
kuàilè

❷ 兴奋 | excited
xīngfèn

❸ 精力充沛 | energetic
jīnglì-chōngpèi

❹ 惊讶 | surprised
jīngyà

❺ 生气 | angry
shēngqì

❻ 尴尬 | embarrassed
gāngà

❼ 害羞 | shy
hàixiū

❽ 紧张 | nervous
jǐnzhāng

❾ 微笑 | smiling
wēixiào

❿ 笑 | laughing
xiào

⓫ 哭 | crying
kū

⓬ 疲倦 | tired
píjuàn

❶ 摔跤 | fall flat
shuāijiāo | on (one's) back

❷ 跌倒 | fall
diēdǎo

❸ 站 | stand
zhàn

❹ 跪 | kneel
guì

❺ 蹲 | squat
dūn

❻ 倒立 | do a
dàolì | handstand

❼ 走 | walk
zǒu

❽ 爬 | crawl
pá

❾ 跳 | jump
tiào

❿ 踢 | kick
tī

⓫ 坐 | sit
zuò

⓬ 躺 | lie down
tǎng

⓭ 趴 | lie face down
pā

⓮ 背 | carry (something) on (one's) back
bēi

⓯ 伸懒腰 | stretch
shēnlǎnyāo

1 十字转门 | turnstile
shízì zhuànmén

2 冷冻食品 | frozen food
lěngdòng shípǐn

3 乳制品 | dairy products
rǔzhìpǐn

4 饮料 | beverages
yǐnliào

5 罐头(食品) | canned food
guàntou(shípǐn)

6 包装食品 | packaged food
bāozhuāng shípǐn

7 面包 | bread
miànbāo

8 零食 | snacks
língshí

9 购物袋儿 | shopping bag
gòuwùdàir

10 试吃品 | free sample
shìchīpǐn

11 肉类 | meat
ròulèi

12 海鲜 | seafood
hǎixiān

13 篮子 | basket
lánzi

14 蔬菜 | vegetables
shūcài

15 水果 | fruit
shuǐguǒ

16 顾客 | customer
gùkè

17 手推车 | cart
shǒutuīchē

18 收款机 | cash register
shōukuǎnjī

19 条形码 tiáoxíngmǎ | scanner
扫描仪 sǎomiáoyí

20 收银员 | cashier
shōuyínyuán

21 塑料袋儿 | plastic bag
sùliàodàir

22 现金 | cash
xiànjīn

23 收据 | receipt
shōujù

24 资源 zīyuán | recycling bin
回收桶 huíshōutǒng

25 熟食 | deli food
shúshí

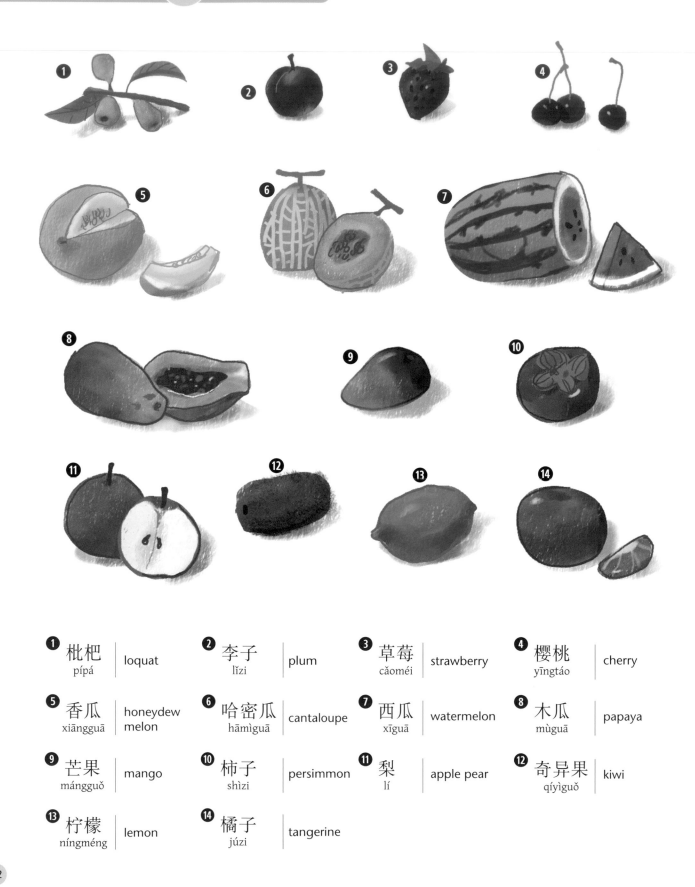

❶ 枇杷 | loquat
pípá

❷ 李子 | plum
lǐzi

❸ 草莓 | strawberry
cǎoméi

❹ 樱桃 | cherry
yīngtáo

❺ 香瓜 | honeydew melon
xiāngguā

❻ 哈密瓜 | cantaloupe
hāmìguā

❼ 西瓜 | watermelon
xīguā

❽ 木瓜 | papaya
mùguā

❾ 芒果 | mango
mángguǒ

❿ 柿子 | persimmon
shìzi

⓫ 梨 | apple pear
lí

⓬ 奇异果 | kiwi
qíyìguǒ

⓭ 柠檬 | lemon
níngméng

⓮ 橘子 | tangerine
júzi

⑮ 橙子 chéngzi	orange	⑯ 葡萄柚 pútáoyòu	grapefruit	⑰ 葡萄 pútáo	grapes	⑱ 杨桃 yángtáo	starfruit
⑲ 苹果 píngguǒ	apple	⑳ 香蕉 xiāngjiāo	banana	㉑ 莲雾 liánwù	wax apple	㉒ 番石榴 fānshíliu	guava
㉓ 荔枝 lìzhī	lychee	㉔ 龙眼 lóngyǎn	longan	㉕ 榴莲 liúlián	durian	㉖ 菠萝 bōluó	pineapple

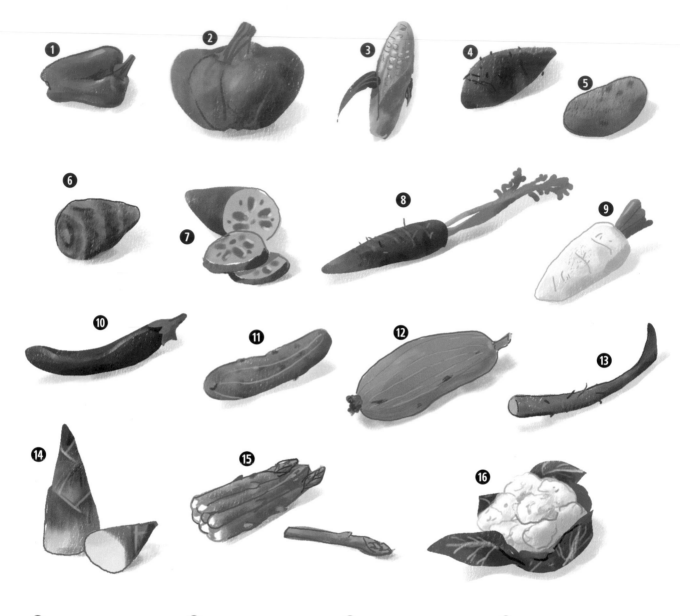

❶ 青椒 green pepper
qīngjiāo

❷ 南瓜 pumpkin
nánguā

❸ 玉米 corn
yùmǐ

❹ 番薯 / 地瓜 sweet potato
fānshǔ / dìguā

❺ 马铃薯 potato
mǎlíngshǔ

❻ 芋头 taro
yùtou

❼ 莲藕 lotus root
lián'ǒu

❽ 胡萝卜 carrot
húluóbo

❾ 白萝卜 radish
báiluóbo

❿ 茄子 eggplant
qiézi

⓫ 黄瓜 cucumber
huángguā

⓬ 丝瓜 loofah
sīguā

⓭ 牛蒡 burdock
niúbàng

⓮ 竹笋 bamboo shoot
zhúsǔn

⓯ 芦笋 asparagus
lúsǔn

⓰ 花椰菜 cauliflower
huāyēcài

⑰ 卷心菜 | cabbage
juǎnxīncài

⑱ 生菜 | lettuce
shēngcài

⑲ 大白菜 | Chinese cabbage
dàbáicài

⑳ 豆芽菜 | bean sprouts
dòuyácài

㉑ 芥兰 | Chinese kale
jièlán

㉒ 空心菜 | water spinach
kōngxīncài

㉓ 蘑菇 | mushrooms
mógu

㉔ 蕃茄 | tomato
fānqié

㉕ 芹菜 | celery
qíncài

㉖ 洋葱 | onion
yángcōng

㉗ 葱 | green onions
cōng

㉘ 蒜 | garlic
suàn

㉙ 姜 | ginger
jiāng

㉚ 九层塔 | basil
jiǔcéngtǎ

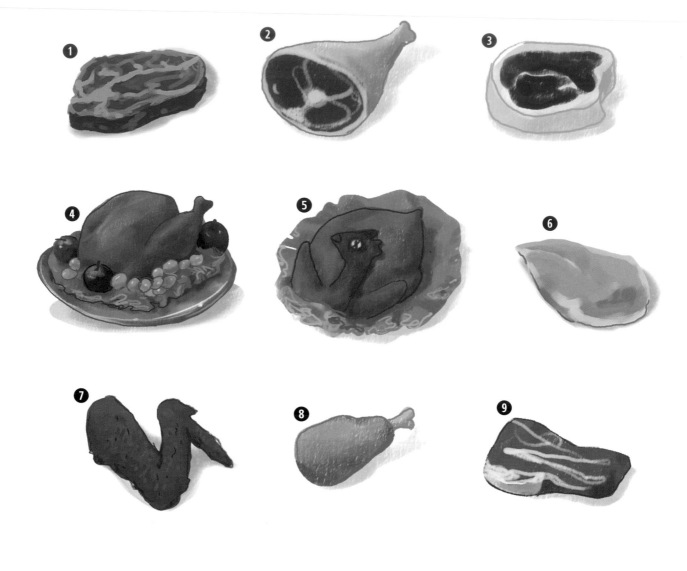

❶ 羊肉 yángròu | lamb

❷ 小羊腿 xiǎoyángtuǐ | leg of lamb

❸ 牛肉 niúròu | beef

❹ 火鸡 huǒjī | turkey

❺ 鸡肉 jīròu | chicken

❻ 鸡胸肉 jīxiōngròu | chicken breast

❼ 鸡翅 jīchì | chicken wing

❽ 鸡腿 jītuǐ | chicken leg

❾ 猪肉 zhūròu | pork

⑩ 肉馅 ròuxiàn	ground meat	⑪ 排骨 páigǔ	rib	⑫ 肉丸 ròuwán	meatball
⑬ 培根 péigēn	bacon	⑭ 火腿 huǒtuǐ	ham	⑮ 热狗 règǒu	hot dog
⑯ 香肠 xiāngcháng	sausage	⑰ 意大利腊肠 Yìdàlì làcháng	salami	⑱ 肉干儿 ròugānr	jerky

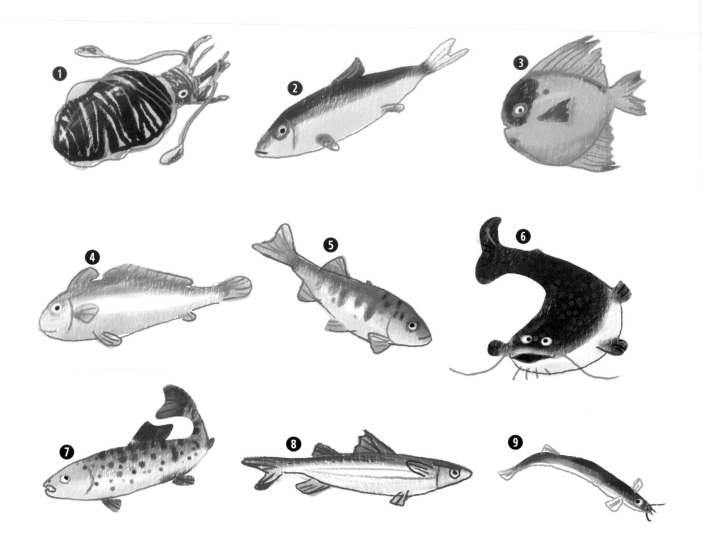

① 墨鱼
mòyú | cuttlefish

② 遮目鱼
zhēmùyú | milkfish

③ 鲳鱼
chāngyú | pomfret

④ 黄鱼
huángyú | yellow croaker

⑤ 鳟鱼
zūnyú | trout

⑥ 鲶鱼
niǎnyú | catfish

⑦ 石斑鱼
shíbānyú | grouper

⑧ 乌鱼
wūyú | gray mullet

⑨ 泥鳅
níqiū | loach

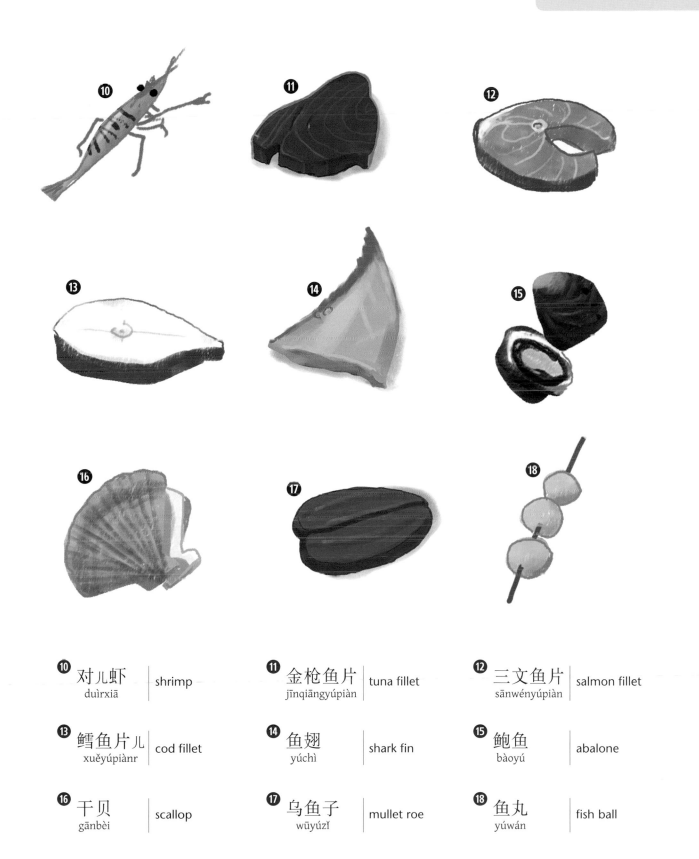

⑩ 对儿虾 | shrimp
duìrxiā

⑪ 金枪鱼片 | tuna fillet
jīnqiāngyúpiàn

⑫ 三文鱼片 | salmon fillet
sānwényúpiàn

⑬ 鳕鱼片儿 | cod fillet
xuěyúpiànr

⑭ 鱼翅 | shark fin
yúchì

⑮ 鲍鱼 | abalone
bàoyú

⑯ 干贝 | scallop
gānbèi

⑰ 乌鱼子 | mullet roe
wūyúzǐ

⑱ 鱼丸 | fish ball
yúwán

❶ 可乐 | cola
kělè

❷ 沙士 | root beer
shāshì

❸ 汽水 | soda
qìshuǐ

❹ 冰沙 | smoothie
bīngshā

❺ 咖啡 | coffee
kāfēi

❻ 热巧克力 | hot chocolate
rèqiǎokèlì

❼ 乌龙茶 | oolong tea
wūlóngchá

❽ 绿茶 | green tea
lǜchá

❾ 冰红茶 | iced tea
bīnghóngchá

❿ 奶茶 nǎichá	milk tea	⓫ 珍珠奶茶 zhēnzhū nǎichá	bubble milk tea	⓬ 牛奶 niúnǎi	milk
⓭ 豆浆 dòujiāng	soybean milk	⓮ 米浆 mǐjiāng	brown rice milk	⓯ 有机饮料 yǒujī yǐnliào	organic drink
⓰ 矿泉水 kuàngquánshuǐ	mineral water	⓱ 柠檬水 níngméngshuǐ	lemonade	⓲ 果汁 guǒzhī	juice

① 黄油 | butter
huángyóu

② 奶油 | cream
nǎiyóu

③ 冰淇淋 | ice cream
bīngqílín

④ 雪糕 | frozen treat
xuěgāo

⑤ 奶酪 | cheese
nǎilào

⑥ 酸奶 | yogurt /
suānnǎi   drinking yogurt /
frozen yogurt

⑦ 生奶油 | whipped cream
shēngnǎiyóu

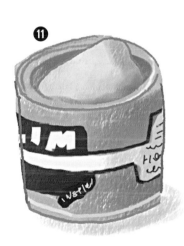

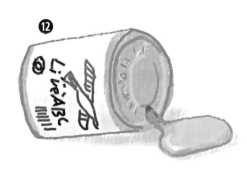

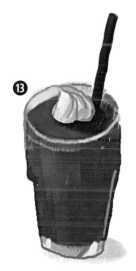

⑧ 低脂牛奶 low-fat milk
dīzhī niúnǎi

⑨ 脱脂牛奶 skim milk
tuōzhī niúnǎi

⑩ 全脂牛奶 whole milk
quánzhī niúnǎi

⑪ 奶粉 powdered milk
nǎifěn

⑫ 炼乳 condensed milk
liànrǔ

⑬ 奶昔 milk shake
nǎixí

① 酸黄瓜　| pickles
suānhuángguā

② 餐巾纸／纸巾　| paper napkins
cānjīnzhǐ ／ zhǐjīn

③ 吸管　| straw
xīguǎn

④ 打包袋　| doggie bag
dǎbāodài

⑤ 煎饼　| pancakes
jiānbǐng

⑥ 鸡块儿　| chicken nuggets
jīkuàir

⑦ 甜甜圈　| doughnuts
tiántiánquān

⑧ 洋葱圈　| onion rings
yángcōngquān

⑨ 牛角面包　| croissant
niújiǎo miànbāo

⑩ 带走　| to go
dàizǒu

⑪ 凳子　| stool
dèngzi

⑫ 汉堡　| hamburger
hànbǎo

⑬ 在这儿吃
zài zhèr chī | for here

⑭ 薯条
shǔtiáo | french fries

⑮ 餐盘
cānpán | serving tray

⑯ 百吉饼
bǎijíbǐng | bagel

⑰ 炸鸡
zhájī | fried chicken

⑱ 松饼
sōngbǐng | muffins

⑲ 威化
wēihuà | waffle

❶ 男服务生 | waiter
nánfúwùshēng

❷ 冰桶 | ice bucket
bīngtǒng

❸ 茶壶 | teapot
cháhú

❹ 咖啡壶 | coffeepot
kāfēihú

❺ 女服务生 | waitress
nǚfúwùshēng

❻ 桌布 | tablecloth
zhuōbù

❼ 菜单 | menu
càidān

❽ 盐瓶 | salt shaker
yánpíng

9 账单 | bill
zhàngdān

10 牙签 | toothpicks
yáqiān

11 餐垫 | place mat
cāndiàn

12 餐巾 | napkin
cānjīn

13 领班 | hostess
lǐngbān

14 柜台 | counter
guìtái

① 开胃菜 | appetizer
kāiwèicài

② 沙拉 | salad
shālā

③ 汤 | soup
tāng

④ 三明治 | sandwich
sānmíngzhì

⑤ 潜水艇三明治 | submarine sandwich
qiánshuǐtǐng sānmíngzhì

⑥ 墨西哥饼 | taco
Mòxīgēbǐng

⑦ 寿司 | sushi
shòusī

⑧ 烤肉串 | shish kebab
kǎoròuchuàn

⑨ 烤鸡 | roast chicken
kǎojī

⑩ 牛排 | steak
niúpái

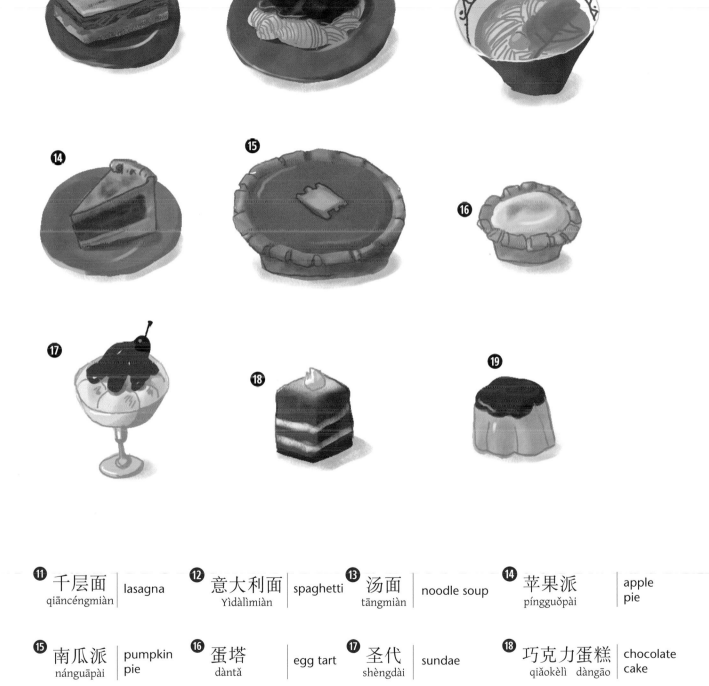

⑪ 千层面
qiāncéngmiàn | lasagna

⑫ 意大利面
Yìdàlìmiàn | spaghetti

⑬ 汤面
tāngmiàn | noodle soup

⑭ 苹果派
píngguǒpài | apple pie

⑮ 南瓜派
nánguāpài | pumpkin pie

⑯ 蛋塔
dàntǎ | egg tart

⑰ 圣代
shèngdài | sundae

⑱ 巧克力蛋糕
qiǎokèlì dàngāo | chocolate cake

⑲ 布丁
bùdīng | pudding

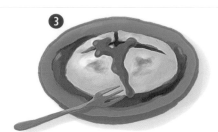

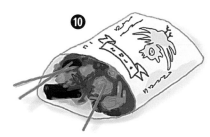

❶ 臭豆腐
chòudòufu | stinky tofu

❷ 炒米粉
chǎomǐfěn | fried rice noodles

❸ 肉圆
ròuyuán | fried steamed meat ball

❺ 鱼丸汤
yúwántāng | fish ball soup

❻ 蚵仔面线
kēzǎi miànxiàn | oyster noodles

❼ 肉羹面
ròugēngmiàn | pork with noodles in thick soup

❾ 卤味
lǔwèi | foods stewed with soy sauce

❿ 咸酥鸡
xiánsūjī | fried chicken with salt and pepper

⓫ 刨冰
bàobīng | ice shavings

Cultural Window

10 Reasons to Go to Night Markets

You can't claim you've been to China until you've visited the night markets there. Night markets are like outdoor shopping malls chock full of local culture. Here are 10 reasons why you can't miss night markets in China:

1. Night markets are a food-lover's paradise. There is an endless supply of delicious edibles everywhere you turn. Some night markets are even famous for a particular dish. Since the portions are small, you can snack on as many different kinds of foods as you like before filling up.

2. If you're a cheapskate, night markets offer bargains galore. After all, who doesn't want to save a buck or two? The rows of colorful stands sell everything from watches to stereos to warm woolen mittens — and you just can't beat the price.

3. Goods at night markets are not only cheaper but also negotiable. Never stop at the price on the tag. Vendors always hike up their prices and they expect to be talked down. It can be a lot of fun to haggle, and it's satisfying too.

4. Slaves to fashion, look no further. Night markets stock the most current fashion trends at the best prices. It's a great place to breath new life into your wardrobe.

5. Where else but at a night market can you sample a plate of exotic seahorses and silkworm larvae? Enough said!

6. When you need a break from shopping and eating, stop off at one of the many game stands. All the classics are offered: pinball, balloon darts, and ring-toss. Sometimes you can win a goldfish.

7. Since you have to walk from stand to stand, you can burn up the calories from all the food you ate — and then eat more!

8. Night markets are good for those of us who like to stay up late and prefer the hustle-bustle of a noisy crowd to staying home. The lively atmosphere will stamp out feelings of boredom or loneliness.

9. Night market food is twenty times better than frozen microwave food from the convenience store, and the stands are open all night.

10. Last but not least, you can practice your Mandarin with vendors at the night markets. Don't forget to use the words you have learned from this book!

---

❹ 卤肉饭
lǔròufàn
stewed minced pork served over rice

❽ 牛肉面
niúròumiàn
beef noodles

❿ 糖葫芦
tánghúlu
sugarcoated tomatoes on a stick

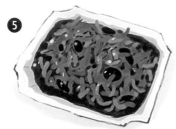

❶ 北京烤鸭 Běijīng kǎoyā | Beijing roast duck

❷ 宫保鸡丁 gōngbǎo jīdīng | Kung Pao chicken

❸ 红烧狮子头 hóngshāo shīzitóu | stewed pork balls

❺ 鱼香肉丝 yúxiāng ròusī | shredded pork with garlic sauce

❻ 麻婆豆腐 mápó dòufu | Mapo tofu

❼ 干扁四季豆 gānbiǎn sìjìdòu | fried beans, Sichuan style

❾ 火锅 huǒguō | hot pot

❿ 点心 diǎnxīn | Dim Sum

⓫ 饺子 jiǎozi | dumplings

⓭ 小笼包 xiǎolóngbāo | steamed pork dumplings

⓮ 酸辣汤 suānlàtāng | hot and sour soup

4

8

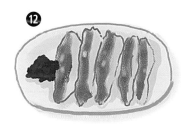

12

4 糖醋排骨
tángcù páigǔ | sweet and sour spare ribs

8 佛跳墙
fótiàoqiáng | Buddha jumps over the wall

12 锅贴
guōtiē | fried dumplings / pot stickers

Chinese Meal Etiquette

Chinese people place great value on what they eat. They do not only put emphasis on the choice of ingredients but also on table manners. Table manners are a vital component and cannot be neglected if you want to understand Chinese culture. Let's have a look at what you need to know while dining and the arrangement of seats.

Seating Manners

The seating arrangement is a very important part of dining etiquette in China. One important concept is showing respect for elders and guests of honor. Normally, the rule is as follows: the left or eastern seat is reserved for the most respected person. This person also "faces the main entrance." After all of the guests have arrived and are ready to sit down and eat, we should remember that the oldest person is usually "the most respected person." Guests wait for this person to be seated first.

Female guest of honor   Male guest of honor
1   **1**
Male guest **2**   **3** Female guest
Female guest **2**   **3** Male guest
4   **4**
Hostess   Host

Things you need to know while dining

If you have a chance to eat with Chinese people, don't forget the following rules:

1. Don't eat until the elders or guests start.

2. Don't drink the soup from noodle soup directly from the bowl, and don't make noise while you are having soup.

3. Don't reach across the table to get food. You can use the rotatable board or ask the people who are close to the dish for help.

4. The bowl should be held and carried upright while eating. Do not put the bowl on the table or move your head toward it to eat.

5. Chinese people use chopsticks while eating. There are lots of rules you should know: First, don't use your chopsticks to gesture. Second, don't touch food with your chopsticks that you are not going to eat. Third, don't stick your chopsticks into the rice. Chinese people only do that to serve rice to spirits of people who have passed away. Fourth, don't tap your bowl with chopsticks. In old times, only the beggars on the street did that to gain attention in hopes someone would fill the empty bowl.

❶ 筷子 | chopsticks
kuàizi

❷ 叉子 | fork
chāzi

❸ 沙拉叉 | salad fork
shālāchā

❹ 汤匙 | spoon
tāngchí

❺ 茶匙 | teaspoon
cháchí

❻ 搅拌棒 | stirring paddle
jiǎobànbàng

❼ 牛排刀 | steak knife
niúpáidāo

❽ 餐刀 | dinner knife
cāndāo

❾ 奶油刀 | butter knife
nǎiyóudāo

⑩ 碗 | bowl
wǎn

⑪ 大浅盘 | platter
dàqiǎnpán

⑫ 盘子 | plate
pánzi

⑬ 碟子 | saucer
diézi

⑭ 水杯 | water glass
shuǐbēi

⑮ 烛台 | candlestick
zhútái

⑯ 蜡烛 | candle
làzhú

① 烤 | bake
kǎo

② 火烤 | grill
huǒkǎo

③ 烧烤 | barbecue
shāokǎo

④ 炸 | deep-fry
zhá

⑤ 炒 | stir-fry
chǎo

⑥ 煎 | fry
jiān

⑦ 熬 | simmer
áo

⑧ 煮 | boil
zhǔ

⑨ 烫 | blanch
tàng

⑩ 炖 | stew
dùn

⑪ 蒸 | steam
zhēng

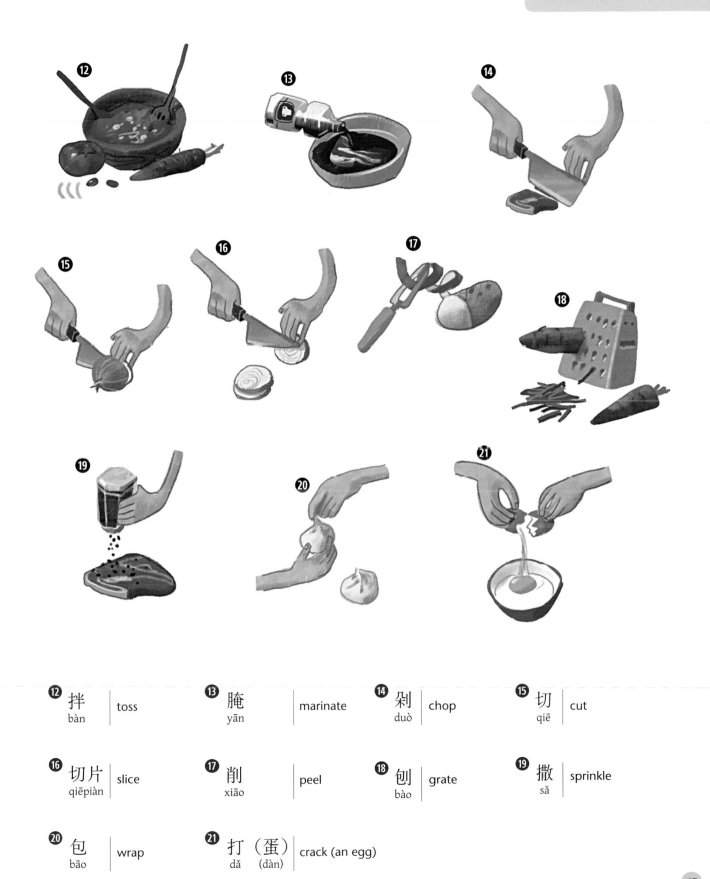

№	字		翻译	№	字		翻译	№	字		翻译	№	字		翻译

⑫ 拌 bàn | toss

⑬ 腌 yān | marinate

⑭ 剁 duò | chop

⑮ 切 qiē | cut

⑯ 切片 qiēpiàn | slice

⑰ 削 xiāo | peel

⑱ 刨 bào | grate

⑲ 撒 sǎ | sprinkle

⑳ 包 bāo | wrap

㉑ 打（蛋）dǎ (dàn) | crack (an egg)

❶ 冰糖 | rock candy
bīngtáng

❷ 砂糖 | brown sugar
shātáng

❸ 盐 | salt
yán

❹ 胡椒 | pepper
hújiāo

❺ 味精 | MSG (monosodium glutamate)
wèijīng

❻ 柴鱼片 | dry bonito shavings
cháiyúpiàn

❼ 醋 | vinegar
cù

❽ 米酒 | rice wine
mǐjiǔ

❾ 色拉油 | cooking oil
sèlāyóu

❿ 橄榄油 | olive oil
gǎnlǎnyóu

⑪  ⑫  ⑬  ⑭

⑮ ⑯ 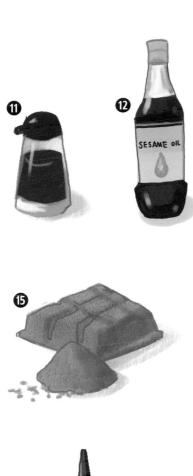 ⑰

⑱  ⑲  ⑳

⑪ 酱油 jiàngyóu	soy sauce	⑫ 香油 xiāngyóu	sesame oil	⑬ 玉米淀粉 yùmǐ diànfěn	corn starch	⑭ 太白粉 tàibáifěn	potato starch
⑮ 咖哩 gālí	curry	⑯ 味噌 wèizēng / wèicēng	miso	⑰ 芥末 jièmo	mustard	⑱ 蕃茄酱 fānqiéjiàng	ketchup
⑲ 辣椒酱 làjiāojiàng	chili sauce	⑳ 沙茶酱 shāchájiàng	shacha sauce				

Additional Information

味噌
wèizēng / wèicēng

"味噌" is a loan word. It's pronounced as "wèizēng" in oral speaking. However, the pronunciation "zēng" does not appear in dictionaries, and some dictionaries indicate that the words "味噌" should be pronounced "wèicēng."

❶ 连衣裙 liányīqún	dress	❷ 礼服 lǐfú	gown	❸ 套装 tàozhuāng	suit	❹ 衬衫 chènshān	shirt
❺ 背心 bèixīn	vest	❻ T恤 T-xù	T-shirt	❼ 裙子 qúnzi	skirt	❽ 裤子 kùzi	pants
❾ 牛仔裤 niúzǎikù	jeans	❿ 短裤 duǎnkù	shorts				

⑪ 四角裤 sìjiǎokù | boxers

⑫ 毛衣 máoyī | sweater

⑬ 外套 wàitào | jacket

⑭ 羽绒外套 yǔróng wàitào | down coat

⑮ 运动服 yùndòngfú | sportswear

⑯ 制服 zhìfú | uniform

⑰ 雨衣 yǔyī | raincoat

⑱ 睡衣 shuìyī | pajamas

⑲ 胸罩 xiōngzhào | bra

⑳ 内裤 nèikù | underwear

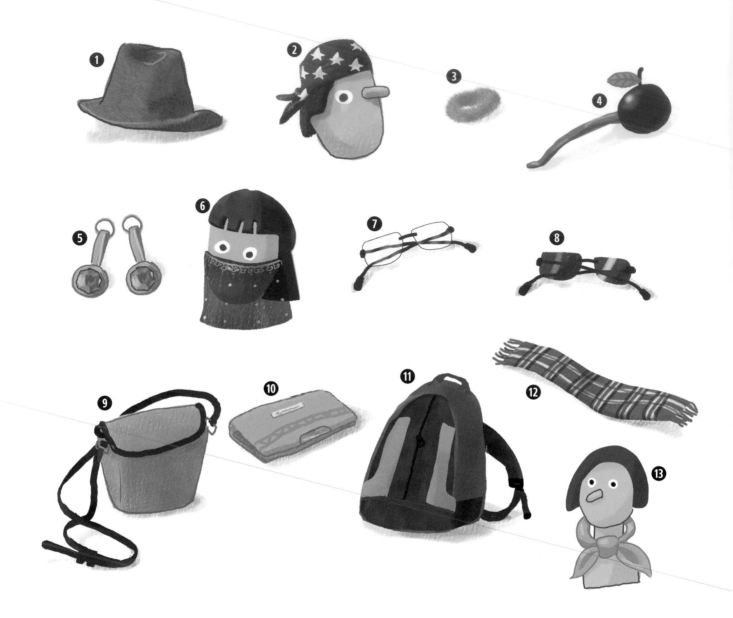

❶ 帽子 | hat
màozi

❷ 头巾 | bandana
tóujīn

❸ 发带 | hair band
fàdài

❹ 发夹 | hair clip
fàjiá

❺ 耳环 | earrings
ěrhuán

❻ 面纱 | veil
miànshā

❼ 眼镜 | eyeglasses
yǎnjìng

❽ 墨镜 | sunglasses
mòjìng

❾ 皮包 | purse
píbāo

❿ 钱包 | wallet
qiánbāo

⓫ 背包 | backpack
bēibāo

⓬ 围巾 | scarf
wéijīn

⓭ 丝巾 | silk scarf
sījīn

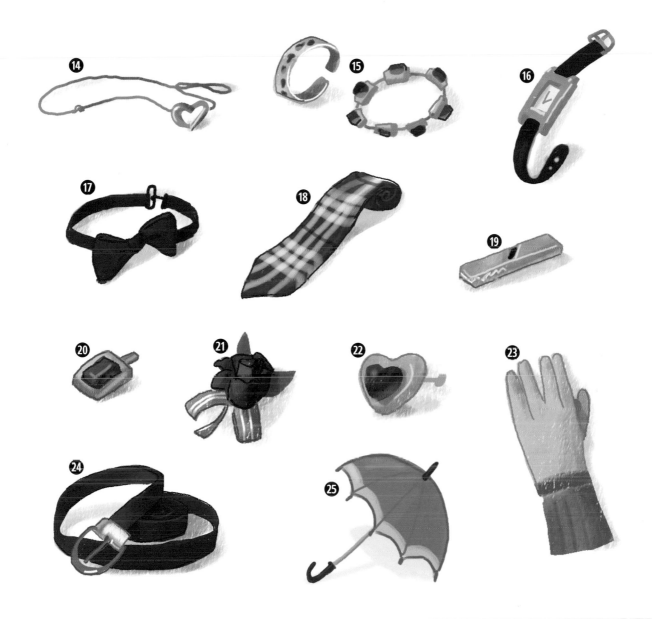

⑭ 项链 xiàngliàn | necklace	⑮ 手镯 / 手链 shǒuzhuó/ shǒuliàn | bracelet	⑯ 手表 shǒubiǎo | wristwatch	⑰ 领结 lǐngjié | bow tie
⑱ 领带 lǐngdài | necktie	⑲ 领带夹 lǐngdàijiá | tie clip	⑳ 袖扣 xiùkòu | cuff link	㉑ 胸花 xiōnghuā | corsage
㉒ 胸针 xiōngzhēn | brooch	㉓ 手套 shǒutào | glove	㉔ 皮带 pídài | belt	㉕ 伞 sǎn | umbrella

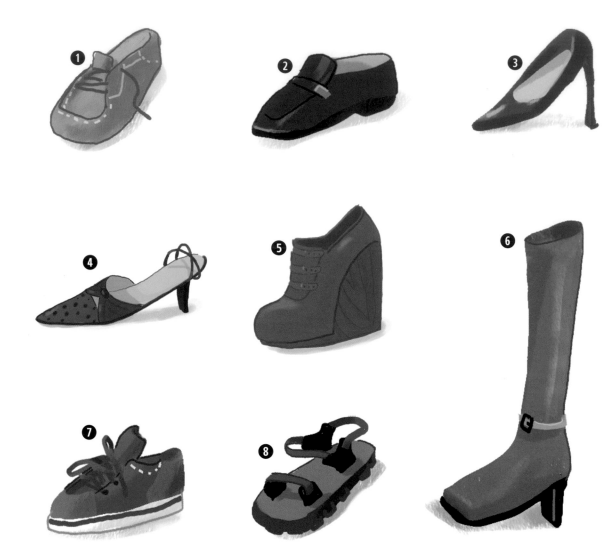

1 鞋子 | shoes
xiézi

2 皮鞋 | leather shoes
píxié

3 高跟鞋 | high-heeled shoes
gāogēnxié

4 尖头鞋 | pointed shoes
jiāntóuxié

5 厚底鞋 | platform shoes
hòudǐxié

6 靴子 | boots
xuēzi

7 运动鞋 | sneakers
yùndòngxié

8 凉鞋 | sandals
liángxié

The Image of Chinese Women – Cheongsam

Cheongsam is the first thing that would come to mind when it comes to Chinese costumes, regardless of whether you are Chinese or not. The cheongsam has become a symbol of traditional Chinese women. Nowadays, it integrates Chinese culture with influences from the West.

History of the Cheongsam

The cheongsam emerged after the Manchu invaded China in the 17th century. At this time, in order for the Manchu government to rule the Han people, many laws were created; one was that all women were required to wear a cheongsam. In the beginning, cheongsam were very simple, loose, and much different than they are today. Near the end of the Qing Dynasty (1644 – 1911), the sleeves and waist of the cheongsam were narrowed. The biggest change to the cheongsam occurred in the 1940s and is attributed to the impact of western culture, when the dresses became even slimmer to emphasize women's figures even more. Today, the cheongsam is worn by women all over the world on more formal occasions and often serve as evening gowns or even wedding gowns.

Fashion Inspiration

Though many people still love the traditional costumes of the past, they are not always suitable for a modern lifestyle. With the cheongsam, for example, the biggest disadvantage is that it can be somewhat physically limiting and cause certain actions to be difficult to perform. Therefore, many changes have been made to make it more comfortable and convenient to wear. Some of these changes have also been made for aesthetic reasons and often reflect a merging of eastern and western fashion design. These new creations can be very popular with young people and considered trendy all over the world.

With the influence of western culture, many western grand designers like to introduce the style of cheongsam into their designs. For example:
- an overlapped collar design with the left piece on top of the right piece;
- a split on the side from thigh to leg.

An introduction of these features into western design has introduced a new fashion trend to the market. Although the cheongsam has become less and less common in eastern culture, the cheongsam design is still a valuable piece of inspiration to designers everywhere, resulting in more fashionable products that combine western and eastern culture.

❼ 中山装
zhōngshānzhuāng | Chinese tunic suit

❶ 百货公司 | department store
bǎihuò gōngsī

❷ KTV | karaoke bar

❸ 电器城 | appliance store
diànqìchéng

❹ 便利商店 | convenience store
biànlì shāngdiàn

❺ 饭馆 | restaurant
fànguǎn

❻ 银行 | bank
yínháng

❼ 医院 | hospital
yīyuàn

❽ 邮局 | post office
yóujú

❾ 自动售货机 | vending machine
zìdòng shòuhuòjī

❿ 饭店 | hotel
fàndiàn

⓫ 健身房 | gym
jiànshēnfáng

⓬ 书店 | bookstore
shūdiàn

⓭ 家具城 | furniture store
jiājùchéng

⓮ 摊子 | street vendor's stall
tānzi

⑮ 酒吧 jiǔbā	nightclub	⑯ 茶馆 cháguǎn	tea house	⑰ 咖啡店 kāfēidiàn	coffee shop	⑱ 药店 yàodiàn	pharmacy
⑲ 电影院 diànyǐngyuàn	movie theater	⑳ 警察局 jǐngchájú	police station	㉑ 玩具店 wánjùdiàn	toy store	㉒ 面包店 miànbāodiàn	bakery
㉓ 美容院 měiróngyuàn	beauty salon	㉔ 熟食店 shúshídiàn	delicatessen	㉕ 消防栓 xiāofángshuān	fire hydrant		

№	中文	拼音	English
❶	邮差	yóuchāi	mailman
❷	邮筒	yóutǒng	mail drop
❸	包裹	bāoguǒ	package
❹	快递	kuàidì	express mail
❺	信件	xìnjiàn	letter
❻	寄信人地址	jìxìnrén dìzhǐ	return address
❼	邮戳	yóuchuō	postmark
❽	信封	xìnfēng	envelope
❾	邮票	yóupiào	stamp
❿	挂号信	guàhàoxìn	registered mail
⓫	收信人地址	shōuxìnrén dìzhǐ	recipient's address
⓬	邮政编码	yóuzhèng biānmǎ	zip code

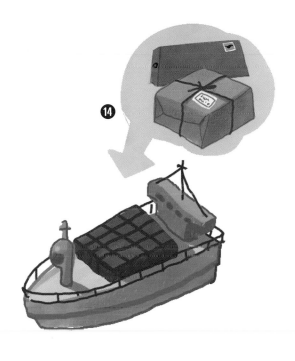

⑬ 航空信 | airmail
hángkōngxìn

⑭ 海运 | sea mail
hǎiyùn

⑮ 明信片 | postcard
míngxìnpiàn

⑯ 报纸 | newspaper
bàozhǐ

⑰ 电子邮件 | e-mail
diànzǐ yóujiàn

❶ 警察局 | police station
jǐngchájú

❷ 便衣警察 | plainclothes officer
biànyī jǐngchá

❸ 交通警察 | traffic officer
jiāotōng jǐngchá

❹ 警帽 | police hat
jǐngmào

❺ 哨子 | whistle
shàozi

❻ 肩章 | patch
jiānzhāng

❼ 警徽 | badge
jǐnghuī

❽ 手枪 | gun
shǒuqiāng

❾ 腰带 | duty belt
yāodài

❿ 警棍 | police baton
jǐnggùn

⓫ 手铐 | handcuffs
shǒukào

12 小偷 xiǎotōu	thief	13 巡警 xúnjǐng	patrol officer	14 警犬 jǐngquǎn	police dog	15 警用摩托车 jǐngyòng mótuōchē	police motorcycle
16 巡逻车 xúnluóchē	patrol car	17 报警 bàojǐng	call the police	18 笔录 bǐlù	written report		

❶ 监视器 jiānshìqì	security camera	❷ 硬币 yìngbì	coin	❸ 纸钞 zhǐchāo	bill	❹ 保险箱 bǎoxiǎnxiāng	safe
❺ 保险柜 bǎoxiǎnguì	safe-deposit box	❻ 窗口 chuāngkǒu	counter	❼ 提款 tíkuǎn	withdrawal	❽ 银行出纳员 yínháng chūnàyuán	teller
❾ 外币兑换 wàibì duìhuàn	currency exchange	❿ 警铃 jǐnglíng	alarm	⓫ 存款 cúnkuǎn	deposit	⓬ 自动提款机 zìdòng tíkuǎnjī	ATM
⓭ 保安 bǎo'ān	security guard						

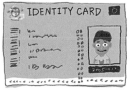

⑭ 运钞车 yùnchāochē	armored truck	⑮ 股票 gǔpiào	stock	⑯ 汇票 huìpiào	money order	⑰ 支票 zhīpiào	check
⑱ 旅行支票 lǚxíng zhīpiào	traveler's check	⑲ 存折 cúnzhé	passbook	⑳ 银行卡 yínhángkǎ	ATM card	㉑ 信用卡 xìnyòngkǎ	credit card
㉒ 身分证 shēnfènzhèng	identity card	㉓ 居留证 jūliúzhèng	residence permit	㉔ 印章 yìnzhāng	official seal	㉕ 签名 qiānmíng	signature

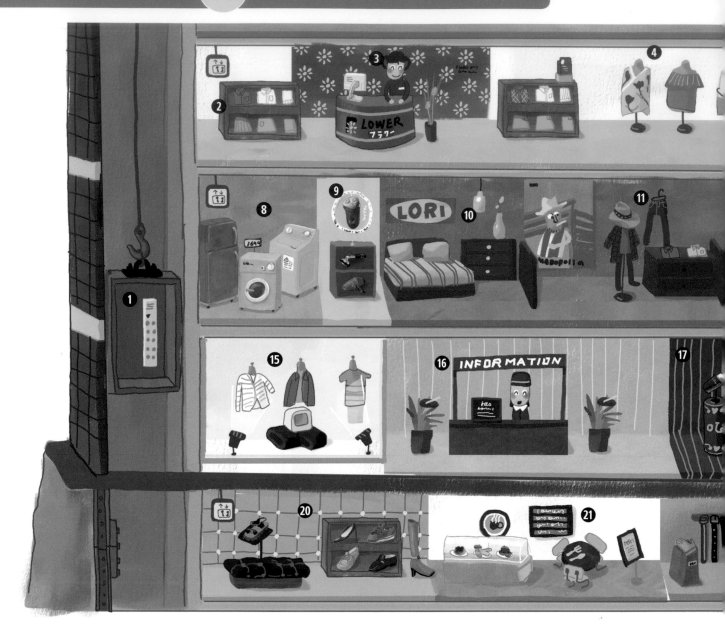

❶ 电梯　| elevator
diàntī

❷ 展示柜　| display counter
zhǎnshìguì

❸ 店员　| salesclerk
diànyuán

❹ 女装部　| women's department
nǚzhuāngbù

❺ 内衣部　| lingerie department
nèiyībù

❻ 失物招领处　| lost-and-found center
shīwù zhāolǐngchù

❼ 自动扶梯　| escalator
zìdòng fútī

❽ 家电部　| household appliances department
jiādiànbù

❾ 小家电部　| home electronics department
xiǎojiādiànbù

❿ 家具部　| home furnishing department
jiājùbù

⓫ 青少年服饰部　| teen department
qīngshàonián fúshìbù

⓬ 运动器材部　| sporting-goods department
yùndòng qìcáibù

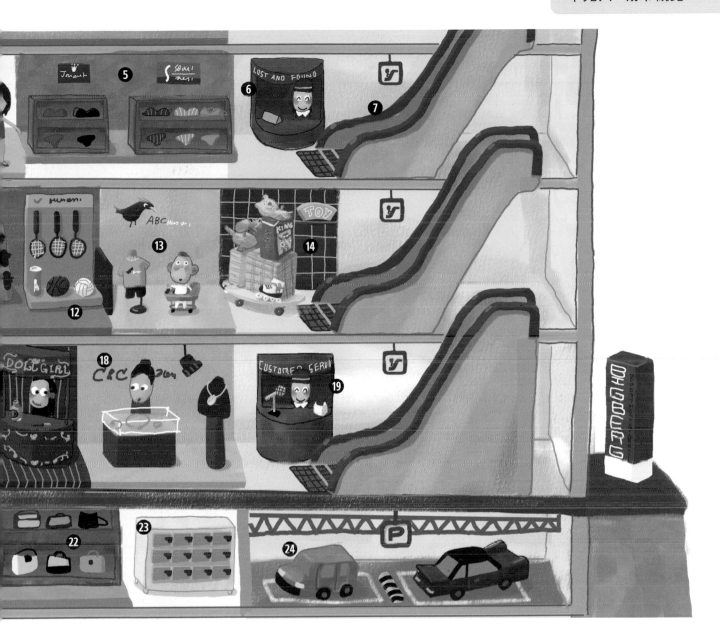

⑬ 童装部 tóngzhuāngbù	children's department	**⑭ 玩具部** wánjùbù	toy department	**⑮ 男装部** nánzhuāngbù	men's department
⑯ 问讯处 wènxùnchù	information desk	**⑰ 化妆品部** huàzhuāngpǐnbù	cosmetics department	**⑱ 珠宝区** zhūbǎoqū	jewelry department
⑲ 服务台 fúwùtái	customer service center	**⑳ 鞋类区** xiélèiqū	shoe department	**㉑ 美食区** měishíqū	food court
㉒ 皮件部 píjiànbù	leather goods department	**㉓ 置物柜** zhìwùguì	lockers	**㉔ 地下停车场** dìxià tíngchēchǎng	underground parking garage

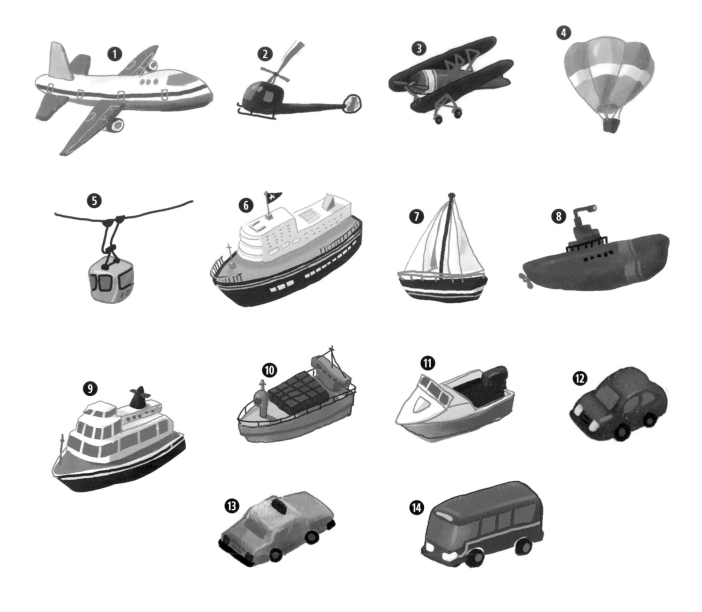

❶ 大型喷气式客机 | jumbo jet
dàxíng pēnqìshì kèjī

❷ 直升机 | helicopter
zhíshēngjī

❸ 双翼飞机 | biplane
shuāngyì fēijī

❹ 热气球 | hot-air balloon
rèqìqiú

❺ 缆车 | cable car
lǎnchē

❻ 游轮 | ocean liner
yóulún

❼ 帆船 | sailboat
fānchuán

❽ 潜水艇 | submarine
qiánshuǐtǐng

❾ 渡轮 | ferry
dùlún

❿ 货柜船 | container ship
huòguìchuán

⓫ 汽艇 | motorboat
qìtǐng

⓬ 轿车 | sedan
jiàochē

⓭ 出租车 | taxi
chūzūchē

⓮ 游览车 | tour bus
yóulǎnchē

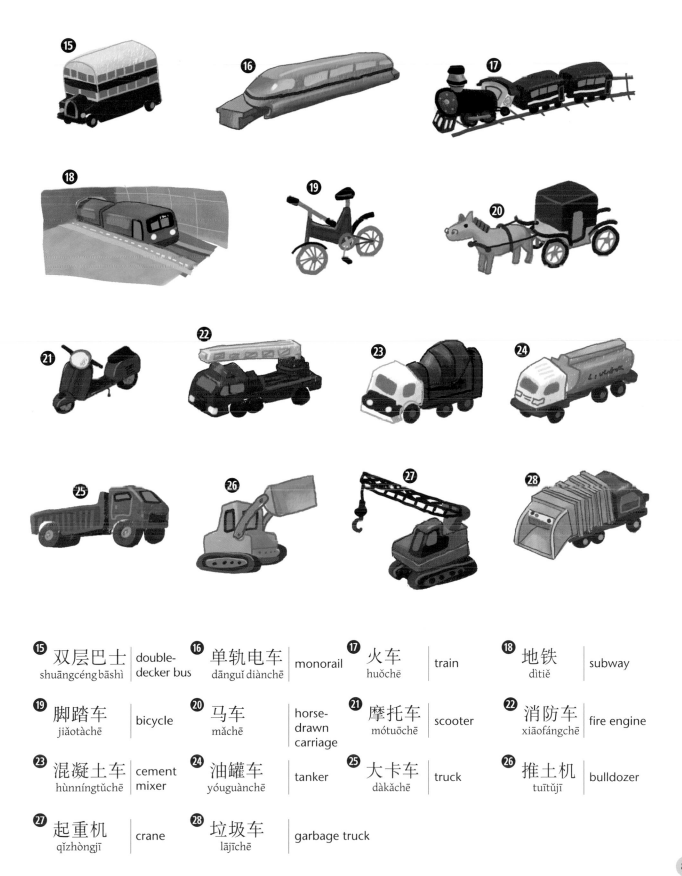

15	双层巴士 shuāngcéng bāshì	double-decker bus	16	单轨电车 dānguǐ diànchē	monorail	17	火车 huǒchē	train	18	地铁 dìtiě	subway

19	脚踏车 jiǎotàchē	bicycle	20	马车 mǎchē	horse-drawn carriage	21	摩托车 mótuōchē	scooter	22	消防车 xiāofángchē	fire engine

23	混凝土车 hùnníngtǔchē	cement mixer	24	油罐车 yóuguànchē	tanker	25	大卡车 dàkǎchē	truck	26	推土机 tuītǔjī	bulldozer

27	起重机 qǐzhòngjī	crane	28	垃圾车 lājīchē	garbage truck

❶ 公园
gōngyuán | park

❷ 天桥
tiānqiáo | pedestrian bridge

❸ 拐角（处）
guǎijiǎo (chù) | corner

❹ 道路标示
dàolù biāoshì | street sign

❺ 地铁入口
dìtiě rùkǒu | subway entrance

❻ 马路
mǎlù | road

❼ 人行道
rénxíngdào | sidewalk

❽ 站牌
zhànpái | bus stop

❾ 加油站
jiāyóuzhàn | gas station

❿ 高速公路
gāosù gōnglù | freeway

⓫ 十字路口
shízì lùkǒu | intersection

⓬ 人行横道
rénxíng héngdào | crosswalk

⓭ 路灯
lùdēng | streetlight

⓮ 红绿灯
hóng-lǜdēng | traffic light

⓯ 骑楼
qílóu | arcade

⓰ 地下通道
dìxià tōngdào | underpass

⓱ 马路牙子
mǎlù yázi | curb

⓲ 停车位
tíngchēwèi | parking space

❶ 盥洗室 guànxǐshì	lavatory	❷ 空中小姐／ kōngzhōng xiǎojiě／ 空中先生 kōngzhōng xiānsheng	flight attendant	❸ 紧急出口 jǐnjí chūkǒu	emergency exit	❹ 遮阳板 zhēyángbǎn	window blind
❺ 折叠餐桌 zhé-diécānzhuō	tray	❻ 置物袋 zhìwùdài	seat pocket	❼ 救生衣 jiùshēngyī	life preserver	❽ 置物柜 zhìwùguì	overhead compartment
❾ 靠窗座位 kàochuāng zuòwèi	window seat	❿ 靠通道座位 kào tōngdào zuòwèi	aisle seat	⓫ 安全带 ānquándài	seat belt		

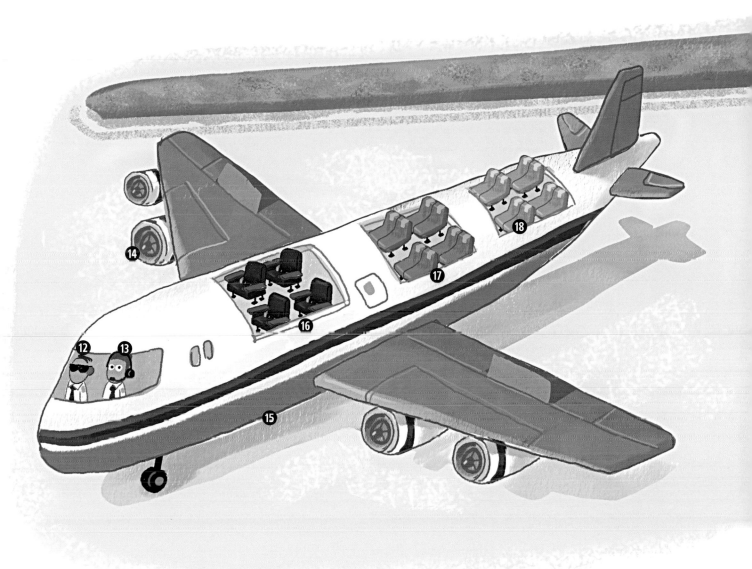

⑫ 副机长
fùjīzhǎng | copilot

⑬ 机长
jīzhǎng | captain

⑭ 喷气发动机
pēnqì fādòngjī | jet engine

⑮ 飞机机身
fēijī jīshēn | fuselage

⑯ 头等舱
tóuděngcāng | first class

⑰ 商务舱
shāngwùcāng | business class

⑱ 经济舱
jīngjìcāng | economy class

❶ 航站楼 | terminal
hángzhànlóu

❷ 外币兑换处 | currency exchange
wàibì duìhuànchù

❸ 保险柜台 | insurance counter
bǎoxiǎn guìtái

❹ 登机报到柜台 | check-in counter
dēngjī bàodào guìtái

❺ 降落 | landing
jiàngluò

❻ 飞机 | airplane
fēijī

❼ 旅客 | passenger
lǚkè

❽ 地勤人员 | airline representative
dìqín rényuán

❾ 航空公司服务柜台 | airline service counter
hángkōng gōngsī fúwù guìtái

❿ 行李 | luggage
xíngli

⓫ 手推车 | luggage cart
shǒutuīchē

⑫ 行李搬运员 xíngli bānyùnyuán	skycap	**⑬ 海关** hǎiguān	customs	**⑭ 出入境** chū-rùjìng	immigration	**⑮ 行李输送带** xíngli shūsòngdài	luggage carousel
⑯ 出境大厅 chūjìng dàtīng	departure lobby	**⑰ 服务台** fúwùtái	information desk	**⑱ 塔台** tǎtái	control tower	**⑲ 免税商店** miǎnshuì shāngdiàn	duty-free shop
⑳ 免税商品 miǎnshuì shāngpǐn	duty-free item	**㉑ 机场巴士** jīchǎng bāshì	shuttle bus	**㉒ 跑道** pǎodào	runway	**㉓ 起飞** qǐfēi	takeoff

❶ 下国际象棋 | play
xià guójì xiàngqí | chess

❷ 下象棋 | play
xià xiàngqí | Chinese chess

❸ 玩儿牌 | play
wánr pái | cards

❹ 打麻将 | play
dǎ májiàng | mahjong

❺ 绘画 | painting
huìhuà

❻ 雕刻 | sculpting
diāokè

❼ 跳舞 | dancing
tiàowǔ

❽ 爬山 | hiking
páshān

❾ 登山 | mountain climbing
dēngshān

❿ 露营 | camping
lùyíng

⓫ 钓鱼 | fishing
diào yú

⑫ 园艺 yuányì	gardening	**⑬ 赏鸟** shǎng niǎo	bird-watching	**⑭ 唱卡拉OK** chàng kǎlā-OK	singing karaoke

⑮ 逛街 guàngjiē — window shopping

⑯ 摄影 shèyǐng	photography	**⑰ 阅读/看书** yuèdú / kànshū	reading	**⑱ 听音乐** tīng yīnyuè	listening to music

⑲ 看电视 kàn diànshì — watching TV

⑳ 看电影 kàn diànyǐng	watching movies	**㉑ 打电子游戏** dǎ diànzǐ yóuxì	playing video games	**㉒ 上网** shàngwǎng — surfing the Internet

❶ 萨克斯风 sàkèsīfēng | saxophone

❷ 长笛 chángdí | flute

❸ 竖笛 shùdí | clarinet

❹ 双簧管 shuānghuángguǎn | oboe

❺ 长号 chánghào | trombone

❻ 法国号 Fǎguóhào | French horn

❼ 小号 xiǎohào | trumpet

❽ 大号 dàhào | tuba

❾ 口琴 kǒuqín | harmonica

❿ 吉他 jítā | guitar

⑪ 电吉他 diànjítā | electric guitar

⑫ 竖琴 shùqín | harp

⑬ 小提琴 xiǎotíqín | violin

⑭ 大提琴 dàtíqín | cello

⑮ 钢琴 gāngqín | piano

⑯ 电子琴 diànzǐqín | electric keyboard

⑰ 手风琴 shǒufēngqín | accordion

⑱ 小手鼓 xiǎoshǒugǔ | tambourine

⑲ 鼓 gǔ | drum

⑳ 木琴 mùqín | xylophone

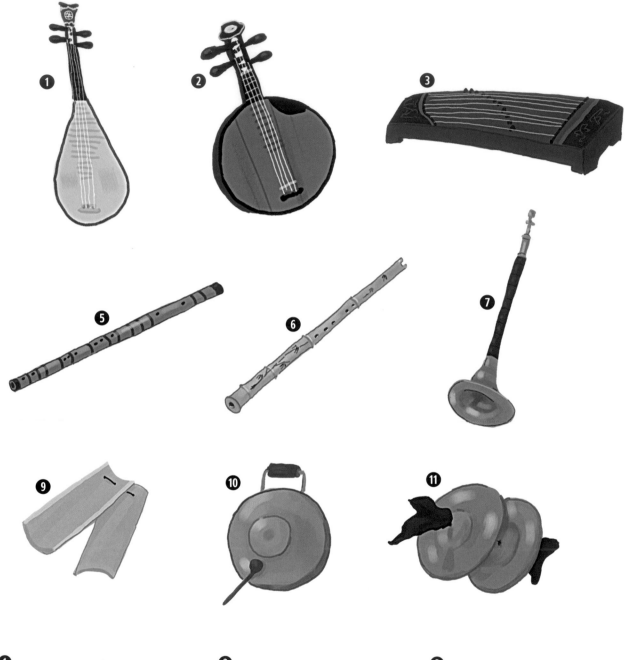

1 琵琶 pípá	Chinese lute (pipa)	**2** 月琴 yuèqín	moon guitar	**3** 古筝 gǔzhēng	guzheng
5 笛 dí	Chinese transverse flute	**6** 箫 xiāo	Chinese vertical end-blown flute	**7** 唢呐 suǒnà	Chinese oboe
9 拍板 / 鼓板 pāibǎn / gǔbǎn	clapper	**10** 锣 luó	gong	**11** 钹 bó	cymbals

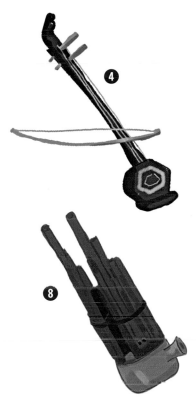

❹ 二胡
èrhú | Chinese violin (erhu)

❽ 笙
shēng | reed pipe wind instrument

❿ 大鼓
dàgǔ | Chinese drum

Chinese Music Played with a Western Twist - The Butterfly Lovers' Violin Concerto

The Butterfly Lovers' Violin Concerto is one of China's musical masterpieces. The concerto was composed by two students, He Zhanhao and Chen Gang, from Shanghai Conservatory of Music in 1958. The Concerto's melody was based on the Shaoxing Opera "Butterfly Love Story." They integrated western and eastern style music by imitating the solo part of the "Erhu" from the opera with a violin. The violin lent itself well to this dismal yet beautiful love story. The Concerto was later arranged into still other versions, such as a piano and a "Pipa" concerto, and was also performed by numerous musicians. If you have the chance to experience it, don't miss the sublime, heart stirring melody of The Butterfly Lovers' Violin Concerto.

A Chinese Love Story

The Butterfly Love Story is a profoundly affecting love story between Liang Shanbo (Liang) and Zhu Yingtai (Zhu). Zhu disguised herself as a man so she could study in Hangzhou. On her journey to school she met Liang, who was to be her classmate. During their three years of shared academic life Zhu and Liang developed a strong friendship. Zhu had romantic feelings for Liang too, but she hid her feelings. After her studies, she returned home. When Liang came to visit her, he discovered her true gender. He was overjoyed and proposed to Zhu, but Zhu's father had already promised her to another man (Ma Wencai). Liang was heartbroken and sank into a depression so severe it took his life. On the day Zhu was traveling to her wedding, she passed by Liang's grave. A strong wind stopped the wedding procession. Zhu left the procession to pay respect to Liang, and his grave suddenly collapsed. Zhu jumped in and was swallowed by the earth. After a while, a pair of colorful butterflies rose from the grave and flew away.

Additional Information: Symptoms

1. 发烧 fāshāo	fever	2. 感冒 gǎnmào	cold
3. 咳嗽 késou	cough	4. 头晕 tóuyūn	dizzy
5. 胃疼 wèiténg	stomachache	6. 头疼 tóuténg	headache
7. 嗓子疼 sǎngziténg	sore throat	8. 牙疼 yáténg	toothache
9. 背疼 bèiténg	backache		

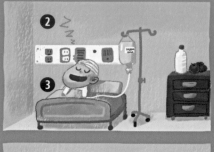

❶ 救护车 jiùhùchē | ambulance

❷ 病房 bìngfáng | ward

❸ 病人 bìngrén | patient

❹ 耳鼻喉科大夫 ěrbíhóukē dàifu | ear, nose, and throat doctor

❺ 手术室 shǒushùshì | operating room

❻ 加护病房 jiāhù bìngfáng | ICU

❼ 牙科大夫 yákē dàifu | dentist

❽ 儿科大夫 érkē dàifu | pediatrician

❾ 产科大夫 chǎnkē dàifu | obstetrician

❿ 眼科大夫 yǎnkē dàifu | ophthalmologist

⓫ 内科大夫 nèikē dàifu | internal medicine specialist

⓬ 外科大夫 wàikē dàifu | surgeon

⑬ 护理室
hùlǐshì | nurse's station

⑭ 护士
hùshi | nurse

⑮ 拐杖
guǎizhàng | crutch

⑯ 步行器
bùxíngqì | walker

⑰ 轮椅
lúnyǐ | wheelchair

⑱ 挂号处
guàhàochù | reception

⑲ 候诊室
hòuzhěnshì | waiting room

⑳ 药房
yàofáng | pharmacy

㉑ 担架
dānjià | stretcher

㉒ 急诊室
jízhěnshì | emergency room

❶ 钵
bō | mortar

❷ 钵槌
bōchuí | pestle

❸ 中药
zhōngyào | Chinese herbal medicine

❹ 经络
jīngluò | meridian

❺ 中医
zhōngyī | Chinese medical doctor

❻ 把脉
bǎmài | pulse diagnosis

❼ 穴道
xuédào | acupuncture point

❽ 气功
qìgōng | Qigong

❾ 打坐
dǎzuò | meditation

⑩ 推拿 tuīná | Chinese massage

⑪ 膏药 gāoyào | medicinal patch

⑫ 拔罐儿 báguànr | cupping method

⑬ 针灸 zhēnjiǔ | acupuncture

1 小学
xiǎoxué
| elementary school

2 幼儿园
yòu'éryuán
| kindergarten

3 高中
gāozhōng
| senior high school

4 初中
chūzhōng
| junior high school

5 大学
dàxué
| university

6 学士
xuéshì
| Bachelors graduate

7 硕士
shuòshì
| Masters graduate

8 博士
bóshì
| Doctoral graduate

9 研究生院
yánjiùshēngyuàn
| graduate school

10 补习班
bǔxíbān
| cram school

Additional Information: School-Related Vocabulary

1. 公立学校 gōnglì xuéxiào	public school	2. 私立学校 sīlì xuéxiào	private school	3. 校长 xiàozhǎng	principal	4. 董事 dǒngshì	director
5. 院长 yuànzhǎng	dean	6. 系主任 xìzhǔrèn	chairman	7. 学者 xuézhě	scholar	8. 校友 xiàoyǒu	alumnus
9. 新生 xīnshēng	freshman	10. 年级 niánjí	grade				

❶ 运动场 yùndòngchǎng	field	❷ 跑道 pǎodào	track	❸ 篮球场 lánqiúchǎng	basketball court	❹ 校园 xiàoyuán	schoolyard
❺ 铜像 tóngxiàng	bronze statue	❻ 校门 xiàomén	school gate	❼ 布告栏 bùgàolán	bulletin board	❽ 办公室 bàngōngshì	office
❾ 校长室 xiàozhǎngshì	principal's office	❿ 洗手间 xǐshǒujiān	restroom	⓫ 教室 jiàoshì	classroom	⓬ 语言实验室 yǔyán shíyànshì	language lab
⓭ 化学实验室 huàxué shíyànshì	chemistry lab	⓮ 置物柜 zhìwùguì	lockers	⓯ 走廊 zǒuláng	hallway	⓰ 礼堂 lǐtáng	auditorium

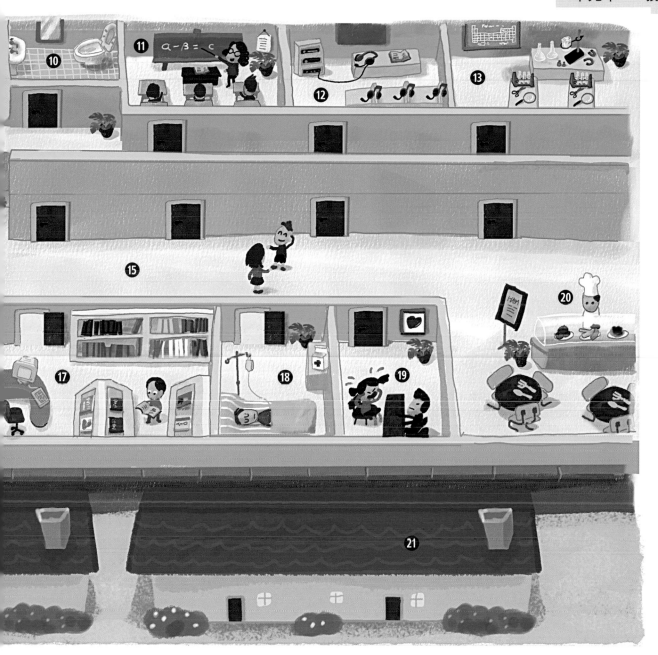

⑰ 图书馆 | library
túshūguǎn

⑱ 保健室 | nurse's office
bǎojiànshì

⑲ 心理辅导室 | guidance counselor's office
xīnlǐ fǔdǎoshì

⑳ 食堂 | cafeteria
shítáng

㉑ 宿舍 | dormitory
sùshè

Additional Information: Sporting Venues			
1. 棒球场 / baseball field bàngqiúchǎng	2. 足球场 / football field / soccer field zúqiúchǎng	3. 保龄球馆 / bowling alley bǎolíngqiúguǎn	4. 网球场 / tennis court wǎngqiúchǎng
5. 高尔夫球场 / golf course gāo'ěrfūqiúchǎng	6. 羽毛球场 / badminton court yǔmáoqiúchǎng	7. 体育馆 / gym tǐyùguǎn	

Part I   Courses · 课程

① 课程表
kèchéngbiǎo | timetable

② 科目
kēmù | subject

③ 中文
Zhōngwén | Chinese

④ 英文
Yīngwén | English

⑤ 日文
Rìwén | Japanese

⑥ 外语
wàiyǔ | foreign language

⑦ 语言学
yǔyánxué | linguistics

⑧ 哲学
zhéxué | philosophy

⑨ 文学
wénxué | literature

⑩ 数学
shùxué | math

⑪ 经济
jīngjì | economics

⑫ 商业
shāngyè | business

⑬ 工程
gōngchéng | engineering

⑭ 建筑
jiànzhù | architecture

⑮ 地理
dìlǐ | geography

⑯ 历史
lìshǐ | history

⑰ 天文
tiānwén | astronomy

⑱ 物理
wùlǐ | physics

⑲ 化学
huàxué | chemistry

⑳ 生物
shēngwù | biology

㉑ 医学
yīxué | medicine

㉒ 法律
fǎlǜ | law

㉓ 政治学
zhèngzhìxué | political science

㉔ 社会学
shèhuìxué | sociology

㉕ 音乐
yīnyuè | music

㉖ 体育
tǐyù | physical education

Part II   Campus Life · 校园生活

1 学期 | semester
xuéqī

2 作业 | homework
zuòyè

3 作文 | essay
zuòwén

4 考试 | exam
kǎoshì

5 月考 | monthly test
yuèkǎo

6 期中考试 | midterm
qīzhōng kǎoshì

7 期末考试 | final exam
qīmò kǎoshì

8 口头报告 | oral presentation
kǒutóu bàogào

9 小组讨论 | group discussion
xiǎozǔ tǎolùn

10 听写 | dictation
tīngxiě

11 作弊 | cheat
zuòbì

12 不及格 | fail
bùjígé

13 奖学金 | scholarship
jiǎngxuéjīn

14 社团活动 | club activity
shètuán huódòng

15 打工 | part-time job
dǎgōng

16 毕业 | graduation
bìyè

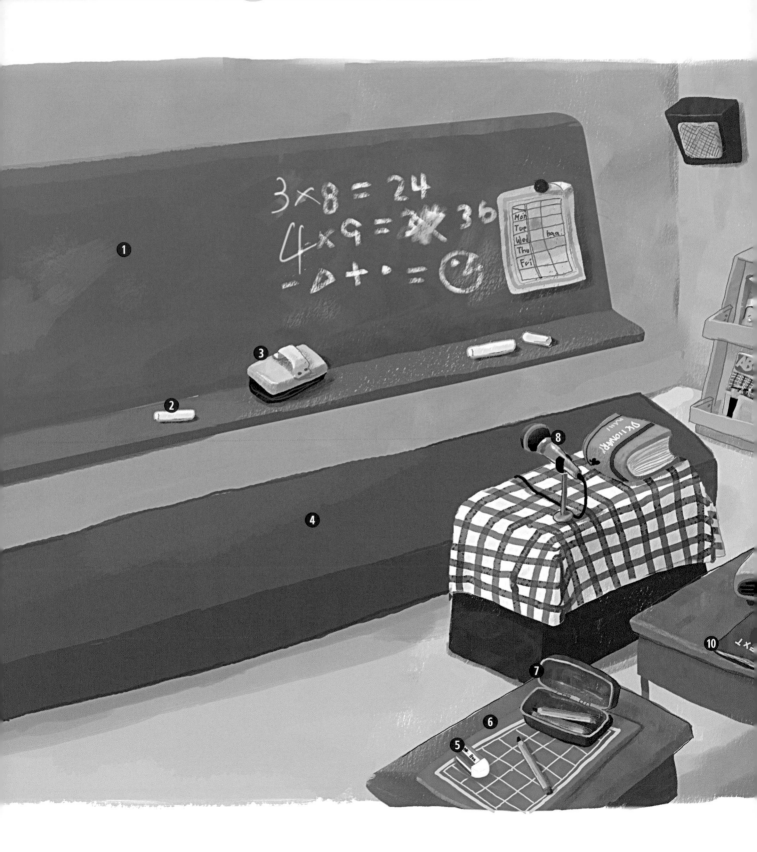

❶ 黑板 | blackboard
hēibǎn

❷ 粉笔 | chalk
fěnbǐ

❸ 黑板擦 | eraser
hēibǎncā

❹ 讲台 | platform
jiǎngtái

❺ 橡皮 | eraser
xiàngpí

❻ 写字垫板 | desk mat
xiězì diànbǎn

❼ 铅笔盒 | pencil box
qiānbǐhé

❽ 麦克风 | microphone
màikèfēng

❾ 投影机 | projector
tóuyǐngjī

❿ 教科书 | textbook
jiàokēshū

⓫ 桌子 | desk
zhuōzi

⓬ 椅子 | chair
yǐzi

⓭ 地球仪 | globe
dìqiúyí

⓮ 地图 | map
dìtú

⓯ 书架 | bookrack
shūjià

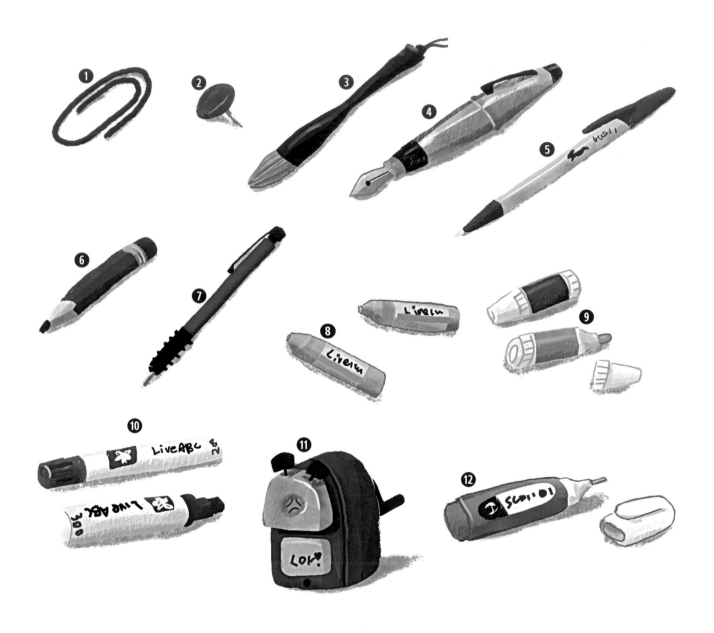

❶ 回形针 huíxíngzhēn	paper clip	**❷** 图钉 túdīng	thumbtack	**❸** 毛笔 máobǐ	calligraphy brush	**❹** 钢笔 gāngbǐ	fountain pen
❺ 圆珠笔 yuánzhūbǐ	ballpoint pen	**❻** 铅笔 qiānbǐ	pencil	**❼** 自动铅笔 zìdòng qiānbǐ	mechanical pencil	**❽** 蜡笔 làbǐ	crayon
❾ 彩笔 cǎibǐ	color pen	**❿** 记号笔 jìhàobǐ	marker	**⓫** 铅笔刀 qiānbǐdāo	pencil sharpener	**⓬** 修正液 xiūzhèngyè	white-out

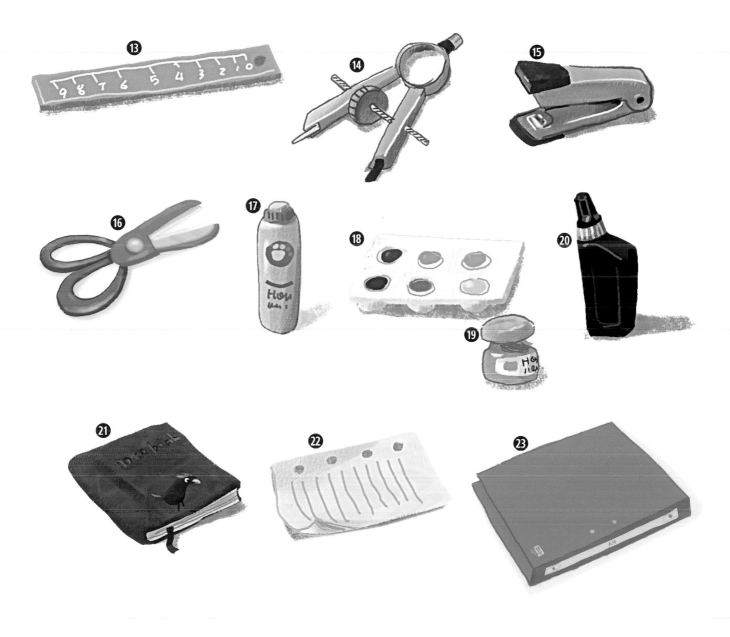

⑬ 尺子 chǐzi | ruler

⑭ 圆规 yuánguī | compass

⑮ 订书器 dìngshūqì | stapler

⑯ 剪刀 jiǎndāo | scissors

⑰ 胶水 jiāoshuǐ | glue

⑱ 调色盘 tiáosèpán | paint palette

⑲ 颜料 yánliào | paint

⑳ 墨水 mòshuǐ | ink

㉑ 笔记本 bǐjìběn | notebook

㉒ 活页纸 huóyèzhǐ | binder paper

㉓ 文件夹 wénjiànjiá | folder

① 红色 | red
hóngsè

② 粉红色 | pink
fěnhóngsè

③ 橘色 | orange
júsè

④ 黄色 | yellow
huángsè

⑤ 绿色 | green
lǜsè

⑥ 蓝色 | blue
lánsè

⑦ 紫色 | purple
zǐsè

⑧ 咖啡色 | brown
kāfēisè

⑨ 黑色 | black
hēisè

⑩ 白色 | white
báisè

⑪ 灰色 | gray
huīsè

⑫ 米色 | creamy white
mǐsè

⑬ 银色 | silver
yínsè

⑭ 金色 | gold
jīnsè

⑮ 深色 | dark
shēnsè

⑯ 浅色 | light
qiǎnsè

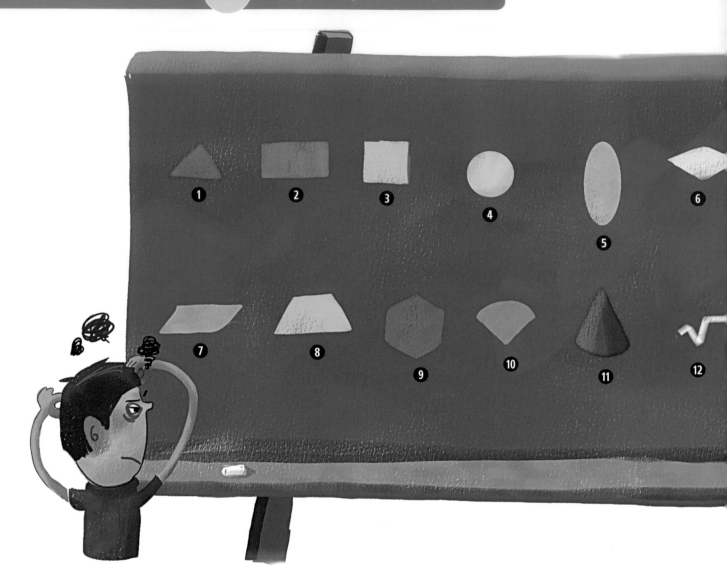

❶ 三角形 | triangle
sānjiǎoxíng

❷ 矩形 | rectangle
jǔxíng

❸ 正方形 | square
zhèngfāngxíng

❹ 圆形 | circle
yuánxíng

❺ 椭圆形 | oval
tuǒyuánxíng

❻ 菱形 | diamond
língxíng

❼ 平行四边形 | parallelogram
píngxíng sìbiānxíng

❽ 梯形 | trapezoid
tīxíng

❾ 多角形 | polygon
duōjiǎoxíng

❿ 扇形 | sector
shànxíng

⓫ 圆锥体 | cone
yuánzhuītǐ

⓬ 平方根 | square root symbol
píngfānggēn

⓭ 加号 | plus sign
jiāhào

⓮ 减号 | minus sign
jiǎnhào

⓯ 乘号 | multiplication sign
chénghào

⓰ 除号 | division sign
chúhào

⓱ 大于号 | greater than sign
dàyúhào

⓲ 小于号 | less than sign
xiǎoyúhào

⓳ 等号 | equal sign
děnghào

⓴ 惊叹号 | exclamation point
jīngtànhào

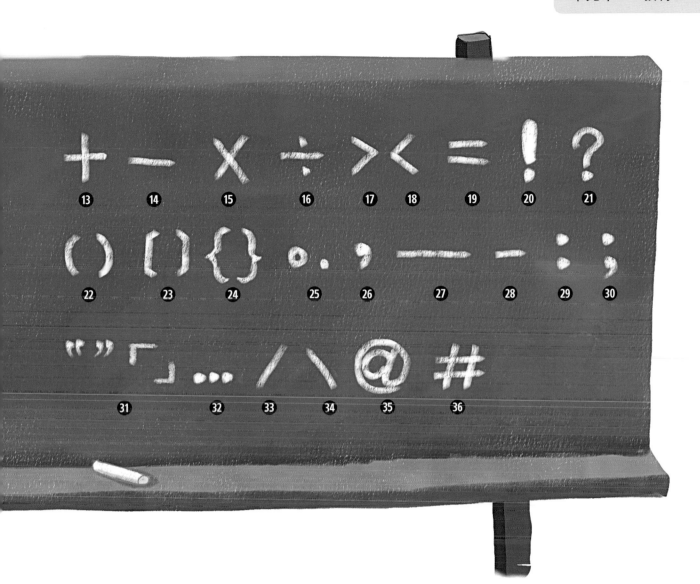

21 问号 | question mark
wènhào

22 小括号 | parentheses
xiǎokuòhào

23 方括号 | brackets
fāngkuòhào

24 大括号 | braces
dàkuòhào

25 句号 | period
jùhào

26 逗号 | comma
dòuhào

27 破折号 | dash
pòzhéhào

28 连字符 | hyphen
liánzìfú

29 冒号 | colon
màohào

30 分号 | semicolon
fēnhào

31 引号 | quotation marks
yǐnhào

32 省略号 | ellipsis
shěnglüèhào

33 左斜线 | slash
zuǒxiéxiàn

34 右斜线 | backslash
yòuxiéxiàn

35 at | at symbol

36 井号 | pound sign
jǐnghào

❶ 跳伞 | skydiving
tiàosǎn

❷ 玩儿滑翔翼 | hang
wánr huáxiángyì | gliding

❸ 划船 | boating
huáchuán

❹ 漂流 | white-water
piāoliú | rafting

❺ 游泳 | swimming
yóuyǒng

❻ 花样滑冰 | figure
huāyàng huábīng | skating

❼ 滑冰 | ice-skating
huábīng

❽ 溜旱冰/ |
liū hànbīng/
滑旱冰 | roller skating
huá hànbīng

❾ 滚轴溜冰 | in-line skating
gǔnzhóu liūbīng

⑩ 射箭 shèjiàn | archery

⑪ 慢跑 mànpǎo | jogging

⑫ 骑自行车 qí zìxíngchē | cycling

⑬ 骑马 qímǎ | horseback riding

⑭ 玩儿滑板 wánr huábǎn | skateboarding

⑮ 单板滑雪 dānbǎn huáxuě | snowboarding

⑯ 滑雪 huáxuě | skiing

⑰ 攀岩 pānyán | rock climbing

1 保龄球 | bowling
bǎolíngqiú

2 篮球 | basketball
lánqiú

3 手球 | handball
shǒuqiú

4 棒球 | baseball
bàngqiú

5 躲避球 | dodgeball
duǒbìqiú

6 高尔夫球 | golf
gāo'ěrfūqiú

7 网球 | tennis
wǎngqiú

8 垒球 | softball
lěiqiú

9 乒乓球 | table tennis
pīngpāngqiú

10 冰球 | ice hockey
bīngqiú

⑪ 曲棍球 field hockey
qūgùnqiú

⑫ 足球 soccer
zúqiú

⑬ 美式足球 American football
Měishì zúqiú

⑭ 槌球 croquet
chuíqiú

⑮ 台球 pool
táiqiú

⑯ 排球 volleyball
páiqiú

⑰ 羽毛球 badminton
yǔmáoqiú

⑱ 板球 cricket
bǎnqiú

⑲ 壁球 squash
bìqiú

❶ 狗爬 | dog paddle
gǒupá

❷ 蛙泳 | breaststroke
wāyǒng

❸ 自由泳 | freestyle
zìyóuyǒng

❹ 仰泳 | backstroke
yǎngyǒng

❺ 蝶泳 | butterfly stroke
diéyǒng

❻ 侧泳 | sidestroke
cèyǒng

❼ 跳水 | dive
tiàoshuǐ

❽ 水上芭蕾 | synchronized swimming
shuǐshàng bāléi

9 滑水
huáshuǐ | waterskiing

10 冲浪
chōnglàng | surfing

11 浮板运动
fúbǎn yùndòng | kickboarding

12 帆板
fānbǎn | windsurfing

13 水上摩托
shuǐshàng mótuō | jet skiing

14 浮潜
fúqián | snorkeling

15 潜水
qiánshuǐ | scuba diving

❶ 掷链球
zhì liànqiú | hammer throw

❷ 掷铁饼
zhì tiěbǐng | discus throw

❸ 推铅球
tuī qiānqiú | shot put

❹ 跳远
tiàoyuǎn | long jump

❺ 跳高
tiàogāo | high jump

❻ 三级跳
sānjítiào | triple jump

❼ 跨栏
kuàlán | hurdles

❽ 撑竿跳
chēnggāntiào | pole vault

⑨ 掷标枪 | javelin throw
zhì biāoqiāng

⑩ 障碍赛跑 | steeplechase
zhàng'ài sàipǎo

⑪ 马拉松 | marathon
mǎlāsōng

⑫ 接力赛 | relay race
jiēlìsài

⑬ 短跑 | sprint
duǎnpǎo

⑭ 百米短跑 | hundred-meter dash
bǎimǐ duǎnpǎo

⑮ 跑道 | track
pǎodào

❶ 西洋剑 | fencing
xīyángjiàn

❷ 剑道 | kendo
jiàndào

❸ 太极拳 | tai chi
tàijíquán

❹ 功夫 | kung fu
gōngfu

❺ 合气道 | aikido
héqìdào

❻ 柔道 | judo
róudào

❼ 空手道 | karate
kōngshǒudào

❽ 跆拳道 | tae kwon do
táiquándào

❾ 泰拳 | Thai boxing
Tàiquán

❿ 拳击 | boxing
quánjī

⓫ 摔跤 | wrestling
shuāijiāo

⓬ 相扑 | sumo wrestling
xiàngpū

1 双杠
shuānggàng | parallel bars

2 吊环
diàohuán | rings

3 鞍马
ānmǎ | pommel horse

4 单杠
dāngàng | horizontal bar

5 高低杠
gāodīgàng | uneven bars

6 平衡木
pínghéngmù | balance beam

7 跳马
tiàomǎ | vaulting horse

8 蹦床 bèngchuáng | trampoline **9** 跳绳 tiàoshéng | jump rope **10** 瑜珈 yújiā | yoga **11** 有氧运动 yǒuyǎng yùndòng | aerobics

12 体操 tǐcāo | gymnastics **13** 哑铃 yǎlíng | dumbbell **14** 举重 jǔzhòng | weight lifting

❶ 老鼠 lǎoshǔ	mouse	**❷ 松鼠** sōngshǔ	squirrel	

❶ 老鼠 lǎoshǔ — mouse

❷ 松鼠 sōngshǔ — squirrel

❸ 袋鼠 dàishǔ — kangaroo

❹ 蛇 shé — snake

❺ 狗 gǒu — dog

❻ 猫 māo — cat

❼ 兔子 tùzi — rabbit

❽ 猪 zhū — pig

❾ 猴子 hóuzi — monkey

❿ 考拉 kǎolā — koala

⓫ 山羊 shānyáng — goat

⓬ 绵羊 miányáng — sheep

⓭ 乳牛 rǔniú — cow

⓮ 马 mǎ — horse

⓯ 斑马 bānmǎ — zebra

⑯ 骆驼 luòtuo | camel	**⑰ 驴子** lǘzi | donkey	**⑱ 鹿** lù | deer	**⑲ 长颈鹿** chángjǐnglù | giraffe
⑳ 狼 láng | wolf	**㉑ 狐狸** húli | fox	**㉒ 犀牛** xīniú | rhinoceros	**㉓ 河马** hémǎ | hippopotamus
㉔ 熊猫 xióngmāo | panda	**㉕ 熊** xióng | bear	**㉖ 狮子** shīzi | lion	**㉗ 老虎** lǎohǔ | tiger
㉘ 大象 dàxiàng | elephant	**㉙ 北极熊** běijíxióng | polar bear		

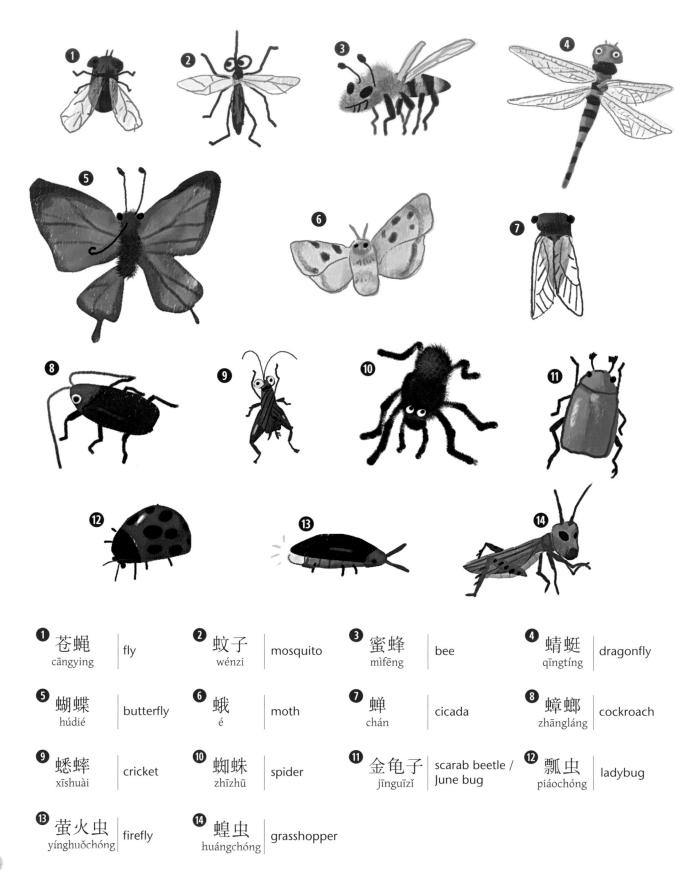

❶ 苍蝇 cāngying | fly

❷ 蚊子 wénzi | mosquito

❸ 蜜蜂 mìfēng | bee

❹ 蜻蜓 qīngtíng | dragonfly

❺ 蝴蝶 húdié | butterfly

❻ 蛾 é | moth

❼ 蝉 chán | cicada

❽ 蟑螂 zhāngláng | cockroach

❾ 蟋蟀 xīshuài | cricket

❿ 蜘蛛 zhīzhū | spider

⓫ 金龟子 jīnguīzǐ | scarab beetle / June bug

⓬ 瓢虫 piáochóng | ladybug

⓭ 萤火虫 yínghuǒchóng | firefly

⓮ 蝗虫 huángchóng | grasshopper

⑮ 螳螂 tángláng	praying mantis	**⑯ 独角仙** dújiǎoxiān	rhinoceros beetle	**⑰ 锹形虫** qiāoxíngchóng	stag beetle	**⑱ 蜗牛** wōniú	snail
⑲ 蚂蚁 mǎyǐ	ant	**⑳ 蚕** cán	silkworm	**㉑ 蚯蚓** qiūyǐn	earthworm	**㉒ 蜈蚣** wúgōng	centipede
㉓ 蝎子 xiēzi	scorpion	**㉔ 跳蚤** tiàozao	flea	**㉕ 蝌蚪** kēdǒu	tadpole	**㉖ 青蛙** qīngwā	frog
㉗ 蜥蜴 xīyì	lizard	**㉘ 鳄鱼** èyú	crocodile				

❶ 鸡 jī	chicken	❷ 雉 zhì	pheasant	❸ 鸭子 yāzi	duck	❹ 鹅 é	goose
❺ 天鹅 tiān'é	swan	❻ 企鹅 qǐ'é	penguin	❼ 海鸥 hǎi'ōu	seagull	❽ 白鹭 báilù	egret
❾ 鸽子 gēzi	pigeon	❿ 麻雀 máquè	sparrow	⓫ 啄木鸟 zhuómùniǎo	woodpecker	⓬ 金丝雀 jīnsīquè	canary
⓭ 白文鸟 báiwénniǎo	white Java sparrow	⓮ 乌鸦 wūyā	crow	⓯ 八哥儿 bāger	mynah		

⑯ 鹦鹉 yīngwǔ	parrot	⑰ 蓝鹊 lánquè	blue magpie	⑱ 巨嘴鸟 jùzuǐniǎo	toucan	⑲ 鹈鹕 tíhú	pelican
⑳ 云雀 yúnquè	lark	㉑ 蜂鸟 fēngniǎo	hummingbird	㉒ 燕子 yànzi	swallow	㉓ 伯劳鸟 bóláoniǎo	shrike
㉔ 猫头鹰 māotóuyīng	owl	㉕ 黑面琵鹭 hēimiànpílù	black-faced spoonbill	㉖ 鸵鸟 tuóniǎo	ostrich	㉗ 孔雀 kǒngquè	peacock
㉘ 鹰 yīng	eagle	㉙ 秃鹰 tūyīng	vulture	㉚ 秃鹫 tūjiù	condor		

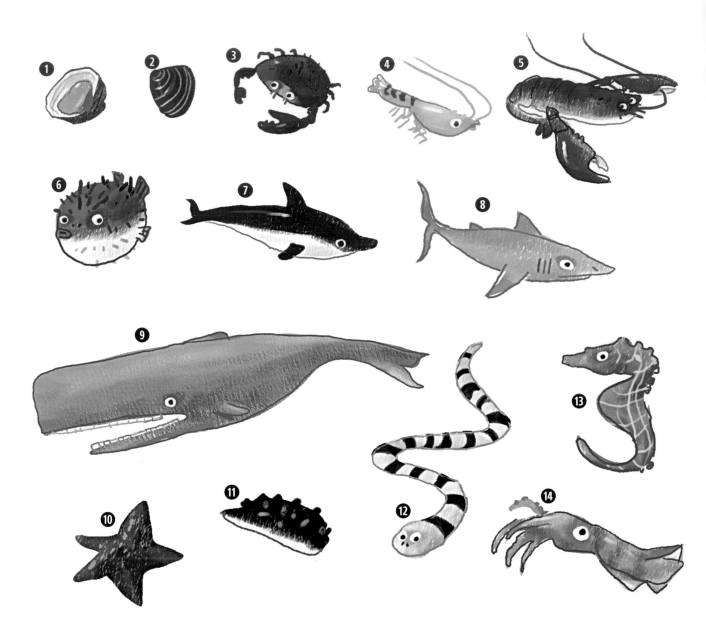

❶ 生蚝 shēngháo | oyster

❷ 蛤蜊 géli | clam

❸ 螃蟹 pángxiè | crab

❹ 虾 xiā | shrimp

❺ 龙虾 lóngxiā | lobster

❻ 河豚 hétún | blowfish

❼ 海豚 hǎitún | dolphin

❽ 鲨鱼 shāyú | shark

❾ 鲸鱼 jīngyú | whale

❿ 海星 hǎixīng | starfish

⓫ 海参 hǎishēn | sea cucumber

⓬ 海蛇 hǎishé | sea snake

⓭ 海马 hǎimǎ | sea horse

⓮ 乌贼 wūzéi | squid

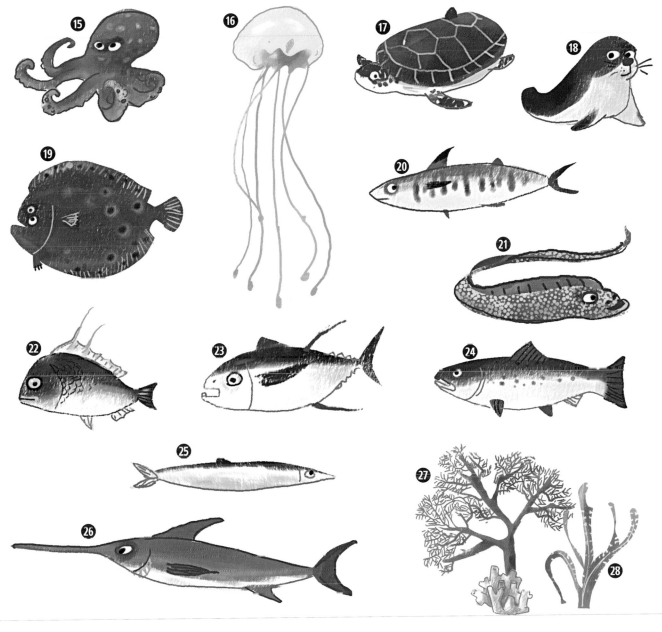

⑮ 章鱼 zhāngyú	octopus	⑯ 水母 shuǐmǔ	jellyfish	⑰ 海龟 hǎiguī	sea turtle	⑱ 海豹 hǎibào	seal
⑲ 比目鱼 bǐmùyú	flounder	⑳ 鲭鱼 qīngyú	mackerel	㉑ 鳗鱼 mányú	eel	㉒ 鲷鱼 diāoyú	sea bream
㉓ 金枪鱼 jīnqiāngyú	tuna	㉔ 三文鱼 sānwényú	salmon	㉕ 秋刀鱼 qiūdāoyú	saury	㉖ 旗鱼 qíyú	swordfish
㉗ 珊瑚 shānhú	coral	㉘ 海藻 hǎizǎo	seaweed						

❶ 水仙
shuǐxiān | narcissus

❷ 杜鹃
dùjuān | azalea

❸ 百合
bǎihé | lily

❹ 雏菊
chújú | daisy

❺ 鸢尾花
yuānwěihuā | iris

❻ 山茶花
shāncháhuā | camellia

❼ 玫瑰
méiguī | rose

❽ 樱花
yīnghuā | cherry blossom

❾ 康乃馨
kāngnǎixīn | carnation

❿ 牵牛花
qiānniúhuā | morning glory

⓫ 熏衣草
xūnyīcǎo | lavender

⓬ 向日葵
xiàngrìkuí | sunflower

13 郁金香 yùjīnxiāng | tulip	**14** 紫罗兰 zǐluólán | violet	**15** 油菜花 yóucàihuā | canola	**16** 蒲公英 púgōngyīng | dandelion
17 三叶草 sānyècǎo | shamrock	**18** 枫叶 fēngyè | maple leaf	**19** 圣诞红 shèngdànhóng | poinsettia	**20** 蕨类 juélèi | fern
21 柳树 liǔshù | willow	**22** 雪松 xuěsōng | cedar	**23** 柏树 bóshù | cypress	

❶ 一月 Yīyuè	January	❷ 二月 Èryuè	February	❸ 三月 Sānyuè	March	❹ 四月 Sìyuè	April
❺ 五月 Wǔyuè	May	❻ 六月 Liùyuè	June	❼ 七月 Qīyuè	July	❽ 八月 Bāyuè	August
❾ 九月 Jiǔyuè	September	❿ 十月 Shíyuè	October	⓫ 十一月 Shíyīyuè	November	⓬ 十二月 Shí 'èryuè	December
⓭ 月历 yuèlì	monthly calendar	⓮ 星期日 Xīngqīrì	Sunday	⓯ 星期一 Xīngqīyī	Monday	⓰ 星期二 Xīngqī 'èr	Tuesday
⓱ 星期三 Xīngqīsān	Wednesday	⓲ 星期四 Xīngqīsì	Thursday	⓳ 星期五 Xīngqīwǔ	Friday	⓴ 星期六 Xīngqīliù	Saturday
㉑ 法定假日 fǎdìng jiàrì	national holiday						

Additional Information: Numbers

1. **1** yī / yāo — one	2. **2** èr — two	3. **3** sān — three	4. **4** sì — four	5. **5** wǔ — five	6. **6** liù — six	7. **7** qī — seven
8. **8** bā — eight	9. **9** jiǔ — nine	10. **10** shí — ten	11. **11** shíyī — eleven	12. **12** shí 'èr — twelve	13. **13** shísān — thirteen	14. **14** shísì — fourteen
15. **15** shíwǔ — fifteen	16. **16** shíliù — sixteen	17. **17** shíqī — seventeen	18. **18** shíbā — eighteen	19. **19** shíjiǔ — nineteen	20. **20** èrshí — twenty	21. **30** sānshí — thirty
22. **40** sìshí — forty	23. **50** wǔshí — fifty	24. **一百** yìbǎi — one hundred	25. **一千** yìqiān — one thousand	26. **一万** yíwàn — ten thousand	27. **一亿** yíyì — one hundred million	28. **0** líng — zero

Note:

"1" can sometimes be pronounced as "yāo." Examples are telephone numbers, room numbers, bus and train numbers, etc. In addition, the number needs to be at least three digits and be pronounced digit by digit. For example, room 14 is pronounced as "shísì hào fángjiān" and room 51 is pronounced as "wǔshíyī hào fángjiān" whereas 101 room could be pronounced as "yāo líng yāo hào fángjiān."

1 太阳
tàiyáng | sun

2 云
yún | cloud

3 雨
yǔ | rain

4 风
fēng | wind

5 雷
léi | thunder

6 闪电
shǎndiàn | lightning

7 雾
wù | fog

8 霜
shuāng | frost

9 雪
xuě | snow

10 结冰
jiébīng | ice

11 冰雹
bīngbáo | hail

№	中文	拼音	English
⑫	风暴	fēngbào	storm
⑬	台风	táifēng	typhoon
⑭	龙卷风	lóngjuǎnfēng	tornado
⑮	高气压	gāoqìyā	high pressure
⑯	冷锋	lěngfēng	cold front
⑰	寒流	hánliú	cold current
⑱	温度	wēndù	temperature
⑲	春天	chūntiān	spring
⑳	夏天	xiàtiān	summer
㉑	秋天	qiūtiān	fall / autumn
㉒	冬天	dōngtiān	winter

Additional Information: Weather Description

№	中文	拼音	English
1.	晴天	qíngtiān	sunny day
2.	阴天	yīntiān	cloudy day
3.	雨天	yǔtiān	rainy day

❶ 新年 Xīnnián | New Year

❷ 除夕 Chúxī | New Year's Eve

❸ 春节 Chūnjié | Chinese New Year / Lunar New Year

❹ 元宵节 Yuánxiāojié | Lantern Festival

❺ 清明节 Qīngmíngjié | Tomb-sweeping Festival

❻ 端午节 Duānwǔjié | Dragon Boat Festival

❼ 中秋节 Zhōngqiūjié | Mid-Autumn Festival

❽ 教师节 Jiàoshījié | Teacher's Day

❾ 情人节 Qíngrénjié | Valentine's Day

⑩ 劳动节 | Labor Day
Láodòngjié

⑪ 国庆节 | National Day
Guóqìngjié

⑫ 万圣节 | Halloween
Wànshèngjié

⑬ 感恩节 | Thanksgiving
Gǎn'ēnjié

⑭ 圣诞节 | Christmas
Shèngdànjié

⑮ 母亲节 | Mother's Day
Mǔqīnjié

⑯ 父亲节 | Father's Day
Fùqīnjié

❶ 高原 gāoyuán	plateau	❷ 森林 sēnlín	forest	❸ 湖 hú	lake	❹ 瀑布 pùbù	waterfall
❺ 山顶 shāndǐng	peak	❻ 山 shān	mountain	❼ 水坝 shuǐbà	dam	❽ 河流 héliú	river
❾ 池塘 chítáng	pond	❿ 树林 shùlín	woods	⓫ 山谷 shāngǔ	valley	⓬ 盆地 péndì	basin

⑬ 平原 píngyuán	plain	⑭ 沙洲 shāzhōu	sandbar	⑮ 海港 hǎigǎng	harbor	⑯ 海滩 hǎitān	beach
⑰ 夕阳 xīyáng	sunset	⑱ 地平线 dìpíngxiàn	horizon	⑲ 岛 dǎo	island	⑳ 海 hǎi	sea

Index